T0328691

Cambridge Elements

Elements in Translation and Interpreting
edited by
Kirsten Malmkjær
University of Leicester

CREATIVE CLASSICAL TRANSLATION

Paschalis Nikolaou
Ionian University

CAMBRIDGE
UNIVERSITY PRESS

Shaftesbury Road, Cambridge CB2 8EA, United Kingdom

One Liberty Plaza, 20th Floor, New York, NY 10006, USA

477 Williamstown Road, Port Melbourne, VIC 3207, Australia

314–321, 3rd Floor, Plot 3, Splendor Forum, Jasola District Centre,
New Delhi – 110025, India

103 Penang Road, #05–06/07, Visioncrest Commercial, Singapore 238467

Cambridge University Press is part of Cambridge University Press & Assessment,
a department of the University of Cambridge.

We share the University's mission to contribute to society through the pursuit of
education, learning and research at the highest international levels of excellence.

www.cambridge.org
Information on this title: www.cambridge.org/9781009165334

DOI: 10.1017/9781009165341

First published 2023

A catalogue record for this publication is available from the British Library.

ISBN 978-1-009-16533-4 Paperback
ISSN 2633-6480 (online)
ISSN 2633-6472 (print)

Cambridge University Press & Assessment has no responsibility for the persistence
or accuracy of URLs for external or third-party internet websites referred to in this
publication and does not guarantee that any content on such websites is, or will
remain, accurate or appropriate.

Creative Classical Translation

Elements in Translation and Interpreting

DOI: 10.1017/9781009165341
First published online: November 2023

Paschalis Nikolaou
Ionian University
Author for correspondence: Paschalis Nikolaou, nikolaou@ionio.gr

Abstract: This Element surveys transmissions of ancient Greek and Latin texts into anglophone literatures, often straddling boundaries between translational responsibility and adaptive, re-creative textual practices. Attention to manifestations of and reasons for versioning, retranslation, hybridity, and translation as experiment compels an introductory discussion of evolving tendencies of classical reception, with particular dispositions relating to a sociocultural context such as that of the United States observed in Section 3. The role paratexts play in the dialogue between scholarship, literary art, and performance is the focus of Section 4, while Section 2 presents readers with a range of English responses to Homer. Creativity through sites and positions of translation is a defining feature of the workings of literary traditions, and of antiquity and modernity, that are in constant dialogue. This Element explores numerous textual manifestations and reasons for invention, along with integrations of thinking on classical translation over the centuries, which have helped shape present-day translation studies.

This Element also has a video abstract: Cambridge.org/ TranslationandInterpreting_Nikolaou

Keywords: classical receptions, Homer, version, translation paratexts, creativity

ISBNs: 9781009165334 (PB), 9781009165341 (OC)
ISSNs: 2633-6480 (online), 2633-6472 (print)

Contents

1 By Way of the Classics
Entanglements of Theory and Practice

This Element surveys ways in which the literatures of ancient Greece and Rome have stayed with us over the centuries in rich dialogue with subsequent writing. A convincing case for the centrality of translation in (re)making literature in the anglophone world is made by Gillespie (2011: 13), who draws our attention to periods that proved particularly significant – the eighteenth century, for example, a 'translating culture, with the greatest prestige attaching to classical translation'. Ongoing interest in studying the intersections of (literary) history, evolving notions about creativity, and cultural self-image is evidenced in our examinations of crucial figures such as Hölderlin in the annals of translation. Hardwick (2003) has done foundational work on a veritable flock of terms – for example, acculturation, analogue, refiguration, appropriation, and intervention – that problematize our perspective on translational dialogues. But classical originals themselves present issues; having been 'endlessly reshaped through transcriptions, copies, editions, commentaries and translations, they have been *reconfigured through generations of different aesthetic and ideological criteria* to the point where it is difficult, if not impossible, to determine what an original might be' (Bassnett 2022: 240; my emphasis). Variations, cultural transfer, and intertextuality already operate in antiquity: forking off from Homeric material, the *Aeneid* represented both a literary evolution of the epic tradition and an attempt at a native, founding myth. Towards the present, literary movements imply concerted action, and *The Classics in Modernist Translation* (Kozak and Hickman 2019) is one of numerous edited volumes attending to how aspects of the classical tradition may be redeployed in validating incipient ideas about literature. Modernists like Eliot and Pound embed stretches of ancient Greek or Latin text in their poetry, and phrasings from *The Cantos* often return to pollinate Pound's translations from Sophocles or Euripides (see Liebregts 2019); the adjectival designation of 'creative' before the word 'translation' registers at least as early as the review essay 'Creative Translation: Ezra Pound's *Women of Trachis*' (Mason 1969).

An essential difficulty in locating cut-off points between translation, imitation, and more transgressive practices may actually bring together theoretical frames and methodologies; Prins (2016: 13–40) explains the necessity of a historical poetics as one that 'cannot separate the practice of reading a poem from the histories and theories of reading that mediate our ideas about poetry' (p. 14), illustrating this through two classically inflected poems: in Robert Browning's 'Pan and Luna' (1880), we see 'historical poetics at work inside Browning's poem, which highlights its own mediation through the transmission, translation, transformation, and reinterpretation of Virgil's lines that compose the legend of Pan and Luna, now recomposed by Browning' (Prins 2016: 21), while in Elizabeth Barrett Browning's 'A Musical Instrument' (1860), Pan turns into a 'questionable figure in an antipastoral poem that interrogates the limit of pastoral conventions' (Prins 2016: 25). We often read ancient texts through the literary productions and artists of the present, relations with which are mutually creative, as Martindale (1993) has argued. Classical scholars themselves compared iterations of ancient plays well before Brower (1947: 383) stated that '[t]ranslations forcibly remind us of the obvious fact that when we read, we read from a particular point in space and time'.

There have been aeons-long entanglements of theoretical reflection with translating texts from the classical world – as in d'Ablancourt's prefaces to the French translations of Tacitus (1640) and Lucian (1654) or von Humboldt's introduction to his 1816 translation of *Agamemnon* – too often involving a spirited defence of strategies adopted or a painful record of compromises that could not be escaped. It is in a preface to a translation of Ovid's *Epistles* (1680; in Schulte and Biguenet 1992: 17–31) that John Dryden illustrates – also through examples of earlier renderings of Virgil and Horace – a tripartite division of *metaphrase* ('word by word, and line by line', p. 17), *paraphrase* ('translation with latitude, where the author is kept in view by the translator, so as never to be lost, but his words are not so strictly followed as his sense', p. 17), and, finally, *imitation* ('where the translator (if now he has not lost that name) assumes the liberty not only to vary from the words and sense, but to forsake them both as he sees occasion', p. 17). Nearer the present, translation theorists build on these foundations, codifying and detailing choices that may be facing all translators: when Lefevere and Bassnett (1998) chart three distinct approaches to translation, we encounter two very old names in a 'Horatian model', which trusts the target audience and largely bases decisions on its needs, and a 'Jerome model', in which favouring the source is paramount, before, finally, the 'Schleiermacher model' is listed, where the strangeness and difference of the source are preserved for the target audience.

The academic study of translation routinely draws material from classical (re)translation. Lefevere (1975) outlines a range of approaches, from metrical to homophonic translation, through English renderings of Catullus' poem 64 that appeared in the course of a century. Scott (2010: 109) produces self-conscious 'scanned readings' of a number of prose and verse translations of the *Aeneid* to discuss 'the ways in which literary translation is a translation *into* the literary' (emphasis in original). Contemporary translation studies returns to further integrate tenets developed in previous decades within a richly interconnected terrain, for instance in Asimakoulas (2019), which combines Lefevere's perspectives on rewriting with aspects of narratology, humour, and reception studies to apprehend a spectrum of actions in rendering Aristophanes, inter- and intra-lingually, for the page or stage or in multimodal reimaginings and adaptations for children.

Re-creative shapes of classical literature may in part be determined by incursions of theory: from post-structuralist challenges to authorship to debates on gender or postcolonial writing. Transcultural strands within gender studies often draw upon translation, with various assertions on the fluidity of sexual identity preoccupied with the influence of language and its power to impose a society's notions on gendered behaviour. Along with a range of interventionist textual practices, translation is seen as challenging binaries, rethought as a subversive force in the work of Levine (e.g., Levine 1984) or von Flotow (e.g., von Flotow 1997). However, Reynolds (2011: 9) warns that we may arrive at senses of translation that exhibit a 'metaphorical drift' in conveying 'an awareness that culture is text and that identity is constructed through language; but they tend not, any more than their nineteenth-century precursors, to hold strictly to the model of translation-between-languages. The word "translate" sometimes means "express again in different words" – and sometimes just "express".'

Post-structuralist theory resonates in studies like Ioannidou (2017) in which humanist and postmodernist strands of engaging ancient tragedy are contrasted, as the author contemplates how rewritings and distinctly metatheatrical adaptations challenge the canon and hierarchies. Such work may highlight questionable morals in the originals and possibly help reclaim tragedy for minority and oppressed groups. Ioannidou pays particular attention to the role of hybrid versions in questioning the boundaries between translation and adaptation, seen as frequently interlacing activities (see especially Ioannidou 2017: chap. 4); she terms 'Dionysiac translation' as one that is resistant to clear-cut distinctions and describes versions of tragedy that, in their treatment of plot, themes, and imagery, 'use their prototypes as fragments of antiquity that can be conceived only in the process of perpetual metamorphosis' (Ioannidou 2017: 128).

But even as theoretical approaches appear productively attuned to practices of classical translation, poets themselves often drive understandings of the art and greatly influence reception dynamics. Stephen Harrison (2009: 15) notes that contemporary poets turn to ancient material

> not so much in a spirit of homage as in a spirit of appropriation. The modern 'deconsecration' of great poetic figures such as Homer and Virgil, in the sense of removing their cultural centrality as canonical and immutable texts generally known and read in their original languages, allows contemporary poets such as Derek Walcott or Seamus Heaney to create new classic works using

classical material and a sophisticated intertextual approach, just as Virgil and Horace created great Latin works through the substantial and subtle reuse of Greek models in a Roman context. Poets can now safely appropriate what they need for their own work and their own contemporary concerns.

Predicaments of reading and reception are poignantly reflected in the poem 'Camilla of the Volscians' by John Matthias (2016: 52–6). After he indicates '*from Aeneid, VII*', over the poem's five pages readers are led into stretches combining critical commentary and (auto)biographical territory. The second section, for instance, begins with the poet recovering a wealth of connections:

> Camilla, blood-sister fore-type of the Roman-slaying
> Boadicea, enters Virgil's Latin hand Englished
> by the generations – Douglas, Surrey, Raleigh,
> Dryden, and the rest . . .
>   she glows
> in language, glows *as* language, bronzed and ready
> for her book, heard by all of them as death-dealer in her
> death-throes all the way to the American Fitzgerald,
> finished with his *Iliad*, done with his *Odyssey*, reading from
> a manuscript, not yet published, to a few of us, friends
> of his friend Sandeen, at Notre Dame, and well before the
> excerpts in *Conjunctions, Kenyon, Poetry,*
> circa 1981–1983 –
>
> 'For Penny,' read the dedication. Penelope, who else?
>
> That was in another age. And when I taught my seminar
> a student even in those days complained: 'What does Virgil
> have to do with our topic, "The Generation of Robert Lowell?"'
> And I said: 'Think about it,' but I don't know that he did.
>
>   (pp. 52–3, lines 24–41)

Yet the starting point for the poem is an actual translation from the *Aeneid*, occurring in a first section of twenty-three lines. Such extraction from the original, and resituating it as a preamble to Matthias' meditation on his colleagues and himself living with the classics, suggests some of the hybrid textual formations that will occupy us throughout this Element. But how can we conceive of this wide array of intertextual relationships, from allusions to rewriting to creative translation, sometimes cohabiting the same page? Hardwick (2011) addresses the question of gradations of classically inspired work and identifies what she calls 'fuzzy connections'. Examining a number of classical transfusions in the poetic work of Patrick Kavanagh, she turns to the palimpsests that emerge as these are subsequently internalized and alluded to by the later Irish poets Seamus Heaney and Michael Longley. The features of these 'fuzzy connections' can be diverse, but they create 'for the reader a simultaneity of experience that brings together the ancient and the new. The ancient image or referent can actually be made into a connector, even if the reader does not have detailed knowledge of its associations' (Hardwick 2011: 56). And she especially considers the effect of translation techniques in several of Longley's poems as incorporating 'the imagist and local/global connections that Kavanagh had made part of the classical poetic tradition in Ireland but … also fulfil[ling] an integrative function allowing the reader to hear the ancient text without previous knowledge of it. Thus allusion, intertextuality and poetic memory coalesce through the activating force of translation' (p. 57).

Several other reasons may present themselves: research on (self-)censorship and its motives when it comes to the classics shows creative ideas coalescing with manifestations of bowdlerization or various expurgations in sanitizing texts to correspond with prevalent mores. O'Sullivan (2009: 76–92) further points out, through examples of translations of Martial and Apuleius, precisely that 'difficulty of differentiation between censorship and naturalization of the classics – a difficulty which is reflected in the contradictions we have seen between the practice and the discourse of a number of their translators' (p. 92).

So literary-creative modulations as well as theoretical stances emerge from attempts to decipher and redesignate classical texts. This Element surveys a transdisciplinary area witnessing manifold penetrations of ancient material into contemporary consciousness and culture. It adopts different vantage points and concentrations: from a case study of Homer translated and reworked, showing epic verse diversifying and rearranged as we reach towards the present; to idiosyncrasies, tactics, or modes relating to sociocultural environs such as those observed in the United States in recent decades; and to reasons for retranslation and paratextual support. Placing the adjective 'creative' before 'classical translation' reflects the often-sizeable adjustments made by the translator in transmitting an ancient text that might still speak to us. But the Element also anticipates tensions and contradictions of a translating act often at its limits, reflecting on itself as we engage with the literary art of the classical past.

Strains, Sites, Shades, and Settings

Particular authors or works, and even characters from classical antiquity that emblematize human behaviour, may rouse modes of translational creativity. These are not merely cultural shorthands achieved through calling upon episodes, or figures from, say, the *Metamorphoses*, or one's stance on sexuality, amplified through referencing Sappho; rather, they may exist as loci pairing up with more concerted, re-creative dispositions.

Pope and Dryden were among the early imitators of Horace's epistles; and revisitings of Horace may also attach to commemorative acts, as when Heaney revoices Ode 1.34 in the wake of 9/11 (see Section 3). With Stuart Gillespie, we discover a selection of translations made by the sixteenth-century poet John Polwhele during the English civil wars and their aftermath that sees 'several of these Horatian poems [used] as vehicles for reflection on the events of [Polwhele's] time' (Gillespie 2021: 54), with yet others clearly signposting Polwhele's relationship, as an artist, to Ben Jonson. Moul (2010) proposes that Polwhele's Horatianism itself is 'Jonsonian' – evidencing 'a habit of Horatian imitation associated with Jonson and his circle' (Moul 2010: 198, cited in Gillespie 2021: 55). A more recent example is Maureen Almond's seventeen recontextualizations of the *Epodes*, integrated into her 2004 collection *The Works* and helping to tell the story of a Teesside working-class community around the end of the Second World War. Almond repeatedly cites *Ars Poetica* in an essay reflecting on her process, and her concluding paragraph reads:

> I hope readers will not see my versions of these Horace *Epodes* as a painting in which the 'painter chose to join a human head to the neck of a horse' (*Ars Poetica* 1–2) but as a work both 'simple and uniform' (*Ars Poetica* 23). So why did I not simply write this collection without any reference to Horace? The answer is that reading Horace helps me to see more clearly those traits which continue to attach to mankind. By recognizing Horace's characters I can more easily understand characters in my own contemporary world, but I believe, too, that this is a two-way flow: 'every interpretation teaches us something more about the content of the interpreted expression.' (Almond 2009: 41; quotes Eco 2004: 12)

Sappho's verse epitomizes the often incomplete state of ancient texts or supports contemplations of sexual identity – in particular, lesbianism. duBois (2015) has delved into ensuing dilemmas for translation, and especially how these may correlate with queer perspectives, dialogues of textual practice, and literary or cultural theory. Similarly, Mueller (2021: 36–52) considers how modern theorists of sexuality categorize the poet from Lesbos. Rayor (1990, 2016) has trained our perspective on the competing inclinations facing the translator of Sappho: from compulsive philological devotion to the remaining text to absences stimulating intervention, a completion via imagined additions. This is poignantly conveyed in Davenport's introduction to *7 Greeks* (1995), which is found to double as a space hosting a translation *that could have been*. We witness, as he engages Sappho, tensions between what is allowed, or the translator's self-regulation, and a finished poem illuminating senses present in the original fragments:

> My intention everywhere has been to suggest the tone of Sappho's words. Had I not accepted as an outer limit to transposing meaning from Greek to

English the rule that one must not tamper with grammatical integrity, I could justify, utterly beyond the pale of scholarship, taking the half-visible imagery of Fragment 119, for example, and, using the multiple possibilities for what the torn words might have been in their wholeness, making such a poem as:

> In yellow frock and yellow shawl,
> Stole of topaz and peach-flower hat
> Knit in your hair like a ring of stars,
> In crocus sash and mulberry vest,
> Sandals red as amber wine,
> You stand in the orchard as
> Delicate as the flowering trees.
>
> (Davenport 1995: 13–14)

He is quick to add that this is 'assuredly not Sappho nor accepted mode of translation' but very likely remains 'an example of her imagery' (p. 14). The list of possible dispositions should include Anne Carson's *If Not, Winter: Fragments of Sappho* (2003), where in attempting to mirror the actuality of lost text, translation becomes more self-conscious. Carson entertains a radical absence for the translator, in moves that may better reveal the state of the original:

> In translating I tried to put down all that can be read of each poem in the plainest language I could find, using where possible the same order of words and thoughts as Sappho did. I like to think that, the more I stand out of the way, the more Sappho shows through. This is an amiable fantasy (transparency of self) within which most translators labor. (Carson 2003: x)

An anthology such as *Sappho through English Poetry* (Jay and Lewis 1996), however, offers a panorama of the creativity instigated across half a millennium, as it tracks literary negotiations of Sappho's style. The editors vividly compartmentalize available material. 'Versions: Translations and Imitations' are followed by 'Representations: Myths, Meditations and Travesties'. I have suggested that, as fellow poets absorb the output of a classical voice like Sappho's in their present, 'any intended work of salvage might very soon approximate tribute, re-imagining or recontextualizing' (Nikolaou 2019: 1). Results of such work therefore can be defined by hybridity or shaded decisively by publication context – or both, as in Lowell's *Imitations* (1961), in which he isolates Sappho's 'Three Letters to Anaktoria' (Lowell 1990: 3–5). If discrepancies in length – the first two poem-letters take up nearly a page each, while a third features only four lines – do not readily suggest what is taking place, Lowell admits in the introduction that 'My first two Sappho poems are really new poems based on hers' (p. xii).

Talbot (2004: 139–69) deems that earlier English literature was less receptive to Callimachus' significance. He deserved more but is already 'ancient history for Propertius and hence doubly-removed from Pound and us' (p. 139) when those 'Shades of Callimachus' are besought in the very first line of *Homage to Sextus Propertius* (Pound 1919). And yet the adjective 'Callimachean' is arguably just as useful as 'Horatian' or 'Pindaric' to describe literary practices of modernity and, as Talbot's examples illustrate, 'T. S. Eliot's hyper-consciousness of literary tradition, or the combination of technical fastidiousness and sensuous erudition in Geoffrey Hill' (Talbot 2004: 140). On these grounds, we are directed to the 1998 translation by Lombardo and Rayor: 'the first English Callimachus to stake itself on drawing out the poet's characteristic self-consciousness' (Talbot 2004: 151) through the word choices and even typographical arrangements the translators employ. Talbot demonstrates the concern shared between Callimachus and modernism to 'make it new' through a translating that seems to position itself 'in a line of kinships that neatly comes back round to the poet himself: Lombardo and Rayor doing homage to Pound doing homage to Propertius doing homage to Callimachus. The interrelationships embody the notion of continuous contemporaneity' (p. 153). An even more crucial inference here is that *both* translations that Talbot discusses, the one by Lombardo and Rayor and the more recent one by Nisetich in 2001, are essentially needed to 'break the ground' because 'Nisetich gives a clear translation, presentation, and scholarly apparatus; Lombardo and Rayor show how Callimachus can conduce to English poetry' (p. 167). 'What is needed now', argues Talbot, 'is for some resourceful poet to make use of these advances, and to reinvent Callimachus in English *in some way that goes beyond translation*' (p. 167; my emphasis). Talbot's review dates from 2004; Section 4 includes discussion of a publication by Stephanie Burt (2020) that is very similar to the likes that Talbot anticipates here. We may perhaps take notice, through the work of Burt and the earlier-mentioned Lombardo and Rayor (1998), of a 'Callimachean strain' in those more self-conscious, creative practices of literary translation.

The response to Ovid is traversed with interpretive, re-creative practices: especially through the *Metamorphoses*, artists across the centuries have intuited an essential meditation on the mutability and illusions that define human life. This epic played a 'major role in the reception of classical poetry in the years from Dante to Milton. First, the process by which classical models are adapted and re-thought in the Renaissance is itself a form of metamorphosis, and Ovid frequently foreshadows this re-use of his work by combining radical change of shape with continuity of certain characteristics' (Mack and North 2015: viii). Shakespeare's Ovidianism is well-documented, and the sway of Ovid in the imagination of later authors has been charted in Warner (2004), while Cox

(2018) has focussed on elements that especially draw female authors. Preceded by notable parodies of Avianus (1993) designed to reflect contemporary realities, Slavitt (1994) translates *The* Metamorphoses *of Ovid* 'freely ... into verse' (as made clear from the subtitle of Slavitt's volume). Although these can be wildly inventive, Slavitt's preface observes a line that should not be crossed in terms of adhering to the original's overall architecture: '[a]s a translator, I take all kinds of liberties, but I am strict in my observation of length and scale, which I take to be significant artistic decisions that any new poem ought to respect and re-create' (p. xi).

Nor is translation theory unaffected, with Levine (1984) drawing on the relationship between Echo and Narcissus, a myth featuring issues of fidelity and subordination in situating the feminist translator as necessarily a 'double betrayer' (p. 92). Equally, literary re-productions of Ovid can be read through the lens of queer theory. Ranger (2019: 231–55) contemplates how Ali Smith's *Metamorphoses*-inspired 2007 novel *Girl Meets Boy*

> also translates, re-translates, and re-writes Ovid's text in a series of queer repetitions. The tale of Iphis informs the narrative structure of the novel, *is re-told multiple times within the narrative itself, and appears explicitly as two consecutive, alternative translations embedded within the narrative.* The first is a paraphrased translation of Met. 9.669–797; the second translation comprises a dialogue over fourteen pages between the two contemporary lovers. Robin and Anthea's polyphonic translation deconstructs discourses of gender and translation by interrupting the act of translation with challenges and questions of interpretation ('She couldn't imagine how she was going to do it ... How do you mean?'; 'Why won't she be able to drink it?'), *and dramatizing within the narrative a fictionalized repetition of the translation performed by Smith and enacted at the level of the book.* (p. 245; my emphases)

Engaging Ovid's work is to oftentimes carry central themes into the very logic and conception of a new literary project, as happens in Zachary Mason's *Metamorphica* (2018), where myths are distilled into the densities of flash fiction, a prose genre that will serve readers in the present – and these intertextual forces are also foregrounded on the publisher's website and in the blurb, which state that it is 'as though the ancient mythologies had been rewritten by Borges or Calvino'.[1]

The collection *After Ovid: New Metamorphoses* by Hofmann and Lasdun (1994) features reconceived episodes by forty-two poets writing in English. The approaches range from close translations to reapplications of an Ovid story to

---

[1] For the description on the Penguin Books website, see: www.penguin.co.uk/books/417694/metamorphica-by-zachary-mason/9780224097970.

contemporary settings and genres, reminding us that 'many of the translations that have established themselves as great poems in English literatures have been energized and shaped by metaphors projected by their sources' (Reynolds 2011: 55). The ambitious volume helps us track instances of evolution or expansion of translation within a poet's *oeuvre*, considering that four contributions by Hughes were the starting point for his 1997 *Tales from Ovid*. A literalist normally, Hughes replaces his own stance on translation with a series of concurrent actions to 'translate, reinterpret, reflect on or completely reimagine the narrative' (Hughes 1997: 36). Eavan Boland's poem 'The Pomegranate', a rewriting of the myth of Ceres and Persephone, is also resituated from *After Ovid* and becomes part of Boland's collection *In a Time of Violence*, published the same year. Trachsler (2021: 38) perceptively notes how

> In the collection context, the reader might identify the poem as a meditation on the ancient myth, whereas its inclusion in *After Ovid* pushes it towards the realm of translation. Through its presence and inclusion in both collection and anthology, the poem seems to remain poised between an original composition merely inspired by a classical theme, and a true rewriting. Its epigraph, however, which only appears in the version published in *After Ovid*, is a quotation from the *Metamorphoses*. This line, quoted in Latin and not translated, draws the poem closer to the original by revealing its precise textual source, whereas omitting this quotation from the version published in *In A Time of Violence* contributes to detaching the poem from its source.

Authors concerned with exile on the other hand are attracted to the *Tristia*, as we observe in instances from Brodsky's poetry written after he was forced to move to the United States or Malouf's re-narration of Ovid's exilic circum-stances in *An Imaginary Life* (1978). *The Word for Sorrow* (Balmer 2009) intersperses translations and versions of Ovid's exile poems with poems often drawing on personal letters and historical documents telling the story of Britain's military engagement in Gallipoli; the two periods poignantly converge and are understood through the story of an old Latin dictionary inscribed to a soldier, which Balmer uses (see Balmer 2005: 60–8; Balmer 2013: 201–22).

Theatrical Spaces and the Global Antigone

In the context of theatre, Minier (2013: 14) admits that it can be

> practically impossible to decide (even with a purely descriptive purpose) how much and what kind of freedom a rewriter/reimaginer is allowed to exercise in order for the artefact to be called a translation rather than an adaptation, a version and so on. Although taxonomies are numerous, there are no objective criteria for the separation of these notions. A great deal depends on what a certain receiving community regards as one or the other at a given historical time.

A double movement for many contemporary receptions is charted by Hardwick (2000), drawing on Burke (1998) – the first, 'de-contextualization, dislocation and appropriation; the second, . . . re-contextualization, relocation, refamiliarization'. More adaptive practices are also bound to occur in a collaborative space where the wilful resituating of ancient characters and plot is often deemed crucial in engaging the audience. Especially for poet-translators like Armitage, a certain ambivalence is felt – as when he relates how workshopping and rehearsals fed back into the text of *Mister Heracles* (Armitage 2000), a version of the play by Euripides:

> Initially, it is an uncomfortable experience to hand over material written in private to a group of total strangers, who then set about it with their minds, voices and bodies, pulling it, stretching it, and on occasion tearing it to pieces. But through a process that included small running repairs on the one hand, to a complete re-threading of plot-lines on the other, I'm sure a more cohesive and comprehensive piece of work has been produced. (Armitage 2000: x)

Compared to more philologically oriented publication environments, theatre can be a reassuring space for (classical) translation work that is applied, variant, and dynamic, as Heaney recognized:

> I declined to do versions of Greek plays for the Oxford University Press series that William Arrowsmith was editing because I didn't know the Greek language. So I didn't feel I should enter the canonical territory. But the *Philoctetes* was for a theater company I was involved with in Derry, and I felt free to tackle it in that context. (Heaney and Hass 2000: 22)

Recourse to one's own lived experience also plays a role in undertaking the project and further justifies licence-taking through a focus on translating 'the overall situation of the play' (Heaney and Hass 2000). Armitage (2000: viii; my emphasis) echoes this climate when stating that what he translated was

> not so much the language as the sentiment and the setting, and the main research tool has been an encyclopaedia rather than a dictionary or thesaurus. It is probably more useful to think that the play has not only been interpreted from Ancient Greek into English, *but that it has been inferred, across time.*

Such language by poets writing today appears to meditate on a sort of leap taking place: a core value in those plays, captured through literary intellect – an intellect that may more likely abstract, omit from, or compress the original.

Receptions of Sophocles' *Antigone*, a play about conflicting loyalties, between the public law and love of one's family, are a rich separate field. First staged around 441 BC at the Festival of Dionysus in Athens, *Antigone* develops into a talismanic text for Western culture towards the end of the eighteenth century, as Steiner (1986: 7) points out. We are also reminded that there can be no 'modern innocence in the face of the classics ... No twentieth-century public or reader comes upon Sophocles' *Antigone* wholly unprepared. The play is unavoidably embedded in the long history of its transmission and reception' (Steiner 1986: 150). This also applies to translators and version-makers. Carson recalls how others before her have read, and staged, Antigone via the lines of a poem-paratext that precedes her own experimental, illustrated version: 'I keep returning to Brecht / who made you do the whole play with a door strapped to your back' (Carson 2015: 3). She pays heed to Hegel's cogitations on Sophocles, both within her own reworking *and* in her prefatory poem 'The Task of the Translator of Antigone', where she also proceeds to reference the opening night of Anouilh's 1944 version of the play staged in Paris, with French Resistance leaders present.

It is a profuse recirculation that also coloured Heaney's thinking when he was invited to do a version for the centenary of Dublin's Abbey Theatre, hesitating initially because

> the play had been translated and adapted so often, and had been co-opted into so many cultural and political arguments, it had begun to feel less like a text from the theatrical repertoire and more like a pretext for debate, a work that was as much if not more at home in the seminar room than on the stage. (Heaney 2009: 126)

In the end, precisely given such 'constant revisitation', Heaney goes ahead: 'The fact that so many other versions are now in existence has become part of the play's meaning' (p. 126). Hardwick (2007: esp. 320–6) further draws attention to how multilingualism in (classical) translations may be the result of ideological and cultural decisions; in Heaney's case, a conscious 'braiding' of strands of English sees him using and developing 'a language with a strong colonial history, English, in a way that both recognized its force in Irish culture and also embedded Irish tonal and lexical qualities' (p. 320). Especially for the Irish audience and its (poet-)translators, this ancient text has come to form an entire chapter inside a literary tradition: a host of critical volumes ascertain the pull the ancient dramatist exerts and proceed to examine transcreations resulting from a particular time frame – in 1984, for instance, we have no fewer than four versions – or from poetic sensibility. There is also research on how someone like Tom Paulin, Marina Carr, or Frank McGuinness positions themselves in relation to Sophocles', Aeschylus', or Euripides' intentions: Irish-specific parameters in staging their plays, shaded by events in the nation's recent history; or certain priorities of implicit comment such as the role of women in Irish society (see, for instance, Macintosh 2016: 323–36; Roche 2020: 12–33).

The 'seminar room' also returns to modulate projects of translation, as in Žižek (2016). With readers given a choice to follow or unfollow Sophocles' ending (in Žižek's iteration, either Antigone wins or the Chorus becomes an 'active agent' and intervenes in eliminating Creon), the event of translation doubles as textual intervention – an initiative that dramatizes interpretations, a conscious redirecting of narrative, possessing and rethinking the plot from antiquity. Žižek (2016: 29) warns that this should be construed as an 'ethico-political exercise' rather than a performable version.

Christopher Logue's 'A Chorus from Antigone' illustrates how often Sophocles' play may transcend theatrical space: first published as 'The Chorus of the Secret Police' in the *TLS* in 1960, it was originally part of Logue's adaptation of *Antigone*, performed in 1960 at the Royal Court Theatre. Sourced from the full version, the chorus leads a separate existence as an item of poetry. As opposed to Sophocles' more even-handed stance, in Logue's appropriation, correspondences of tone and perspective with Logue's political sympathies are notable. What is more, 'A Chorus from Antigone' is revised for inclusion in *Ode to the Dodo* (1982), and more than a decade later is part of the *Selected Poems* (1996) – further steps in a story of gradual owner-ship. By no means is Logue the first poet on a scene of textual extrications and repurposing: in 1849, Arnold produced a 103-line 'Fragment of an "Antigone"'. Poetry also rethinks itself via theatrical translation: Steiner (1986: 70) argues that Hölderlin's *Antigonä* 'carries to extremity the radicalization of lexical and syntactic means, the shift from sequential-logical conventions and from the external reference of ordinary discourse to an internalized coherence of meta-phor and image-clusters, which make of Hölderlin's late work a primary source of modernism'.

Nor should it surprise us that we may come across translation efforts such as David Constantine's of *Hölderlin's Sophocles: Oedipus and Antigone* (2001), endorsing the historical and cultural significance of such idiosyncratic trans-lation. There is a conceptual creativity involved, a reconfirmation of what the original existed as, in keeping close to the 'strange German, in the hope of arriving at an analogous strangeness in English' (Constantine 2001: 13). In a later essay on Hölderlin's practice as poet-translator, Constantine argues that his approach to the classics is creative in the sense of being individually optimized – a result of a classical original understood as a metaphor 'of the translator's idea of the particular project': in Pindar's *Odes* and the two plays of Sophocles that Hölderlin translates, 'there is a transference of lexical sense, but also, just as important, of an idea; and what is involved in that transference varies greatly between them. Three texts, three translations' (Constantine 2011: 90).

Sophocles' characters transcend cultural specificities and geography. Gibbs (2007: 54–71) has paid attention to Indigenous performance traditions of West Africa, exploring inflections on *Antigone* brought through Caribbean and Black Atlantic cultural traffic in an essay that examines dialogues of Ghanaian theatre with ancient Greek plays – for example, in Brathwaite's *Odale's Choice* (1967). In an Australian context, Elena Carapetis, the creator of a recent kaleidoscopic version, points out that '[t]he script starts off as a very familiar rendering of the play, Classical and Greek. But with the stage direction "Two Thousand Years Later" it explodes and splinters into vignettes of the now, where we meet Antigones of today' (among them, Greta Thunberg and Malala Yousafzai), underlining 'the enduring power of the patriarchy and why the voices of the young and queer continue to be silenced and eliminated' ('Antigone' 2022).

The reasoning for modes of creativity as exemplified here is evident in a 'Note on Casting' at the start of an adaptation included in Powers (2021) which reads: 'The cast should be diverse, particularly in reflection of the community it is performed in. The role of Antigone must be played by a person of color' (Kim 2021: 235). Interviewed by the volume's editor and a class of English majors at CUNY in 2018, the director explains that he wanted to explore how a young person gets this immense courage to face the danger of doing what she feels is right. Intentions about language and tone in this case seem attuned to key cultural concerns today:

> It's about her own growing up, and owning herself, and owning her voice. So when I was staging it, I wanted to make the burial a joyful moment, with singing and dance. In [the song] 'Free She' in the second act, I intended to show a progression from her finding her voice to using it. She becomes a figure who's speaking about not just herself but all women around the world who have been oppressed. (Rolon et al. 2021: 250)

In such 'reclaiming', shifts go beyond fused genres and into plot: Antigone commits suicide by setting herself on fire. When asked if there is a 'sacrificial vibe' to this ending, the director mentions Tibetan monks self-immolating and the figure of Joan of Arc, a response illustrative of the layers, recognitions, and analogies time has bestowed on Sophocles' creation, the possible emphases, or identifications that depend on our reading in the culture. Variant intentions are symptomatic of the bountiful variants in existence, to the point where the original, as Steiner (1986: 297) warned decades ago, 'runs the danger of receding into context'.

From the Many Lives of Versions

When process and outcome are both meant to be poetic, Don Paterson (2006: 75) tells us, the ambition must be to go even further back and 'first reinhabit that extralinguistic silence the original poem once itself enjoyed'. Subjectivity and a more interpretative line attach to everything now being subservient to a lyric rule in the case of versioning: 'because you know the original surface-sense will suffer as a consequence of the local exigencies of consonance, rhyme and metre, your allegiance must then switch from the original words to your subjective interpretation of them' (p. 75). The 'version' designation admits the fact of an origin continuously refracted and helps legitimize a literary mode, which steers the response of readers and critics towards a recognition of two sensibilities conversing. We witness this often in publishers' websites or blurbs such as the one found on the back of Hughes' *Tales from Ovid* (1997) that often reach for some impossible duality and encompass a contradiction that ticks all the boxes: Hughes' response to Ovid is argued for as being 'so whole-hearted that he achieves here what only the greatest translators have been able to do, providing not just an accurate account of the original, but one so thoroughly imbued with his own qualities that it is as if Latin and English poet *were somehow the same person*' (Hughes 1997: blurb, my emphasis). Poets themselves anticipate such dynamics: Parker (2019: 100fn) notes that Hughes wrote to Heaney twice on the subject of Antigone, twenty years before Heaney accepted the commission that led to *The Burial at Thebes*; first sending him a translation of the play in November 1983, then, in an undated letter from late 1984, 'he wonders "what you might make of an Antigone"'. There are not that many steps from such settings of intimated confluence to witness creative classical translation as textual intervention: Heaney adds further choruses as Sophoclean *Philoctetes* turns to *The Cure at Troy* and then makes a point of detaching and pre-publishing this work (see Heaney 1991: 131–8). Hughes expands the scene of Hercules' revelry in Euripides' *Alcestis* (1999), interpolates a staging of the hero's labours, past and yet to come, and further additions include a poignant dialogue between Apollo and Thanatos (Death).

Creativity is also involved in how genres, diction, metres, tropes, and passages from the classical past contaminate periods of literature. Henry Howard brings the iambic pentameter into English when he translates Virgil. Cowley's *Pindarique Odes* (1656) metabolize Pindar to such an extent that a mode of English ode becomes popular among versifiers for the next century and a half or so. Moreover, when previous models are engaged, from Virgil to Milton and beyond, a disentanglement of allusion, influence, adaptation, echo, and borrowing can prove an impenetrable problem once removed from the mind of the author. Machacek's (2011) study of intertextuality quickly establishes how Milton draws from not only Homer but also Homer's many classical and post-classical imitators, with works such as *Paradise Lost* permeated by 'phrases from the entire preceding literary tradition' (p. 25). But even when an allusion clearly belongs in the classical period, it is often hard to distinguish whether it is Homeric or, say, Virgilian in nature, or if certain passages and scenes imitated have indeed fused in Milton's mind. Such instances double as unannounced or internalized creative classical translations.

Modernist tenets allow for further embeddings, cuts, and subtle echoing of issues when the poet revisits the classics: as Liveley points out, an extraction from the *Odyssey* (lines 1.1–98) that H.D. includes in her *Translations 1915–1920*, recentres female agency. And it is what H.D. leaves out that holds significance:

> H.D. simply edits out the summary account that Homer gives of the many men and their cities that Odysseus encounters on his travels; she also cuts Homer's reference here to the fatal folly of Odysseus' comrades, along with Homer's second invocation to the Muse as 'goddess, daughter of Zeus' (*θεά, θύγατερ Διός*: *Odyssey* 1.10). H.D.'s fragment cuts the extraneous men out of the story's prologue to allow the *Odyssey's* female characters – the Muse, Calypso, Penelope, Athene – to come in to the narrative foreground. In so doing, H.D. succinctly foregrounds her own focus and interestedness in telling the *fabula* of Homer's epic differently. (Liveley 2019: 30)

Typographical arrangement adds to the creativity of H.D.'s reworking, and since the formal hexameter of the original is abandoned in favour of 'an informal modernist lyric which allows certain key words to stand out in their own lines, the effect is of poem as recovered fragment or reconstructed palimpsest. The missing text cedes prominence to an imagist pattern of isolated words' (Liveley 2019: 28). These strategies remind us of how re-creation may be spurred on by self-reference: 'Athene's speech and her intervention in the affairs of the gods and heroes of the epic world', Liveley continues, 'serve as a potent analogy to H.D.'s own literary intervention here – and elsewhere in her poetic engagements with Homer' (p. 30). There is similar foregrounding and/or inventive editing of classical material when Lowell anthologizes his translation work: under the title 'The Killing of Lykaon', he poignantly joins the first, emblematic lines of the *Iliad* with thirty-nine lines that originate from Book 21 (Lowell 1990: 1–2). The narrative emerging in such collages is not merely thematic amplification, instances of classically sourced 'found poetry', but an implicit registering of the forms literary creativity may take. In the wake of modernism, we come across such poignant isolations of material or an arbitrary foregrounding of dimensions in one's original. Malmkjær (2020: 73) argues through several examples that adopting what she describes as 'the aesthetic attitude to one's source text need not lead a translator to seek to replicate all of its characteristics precisely in translating it'; she adds that Nosbaum (2006: 122) 'made his translation of a passage from the *Aeneid* which deals with the fate of

Palinurus "out of a desire to intensify" the lyrical quality that he perceives in it and which "fixes Palinurus in the mind"' (Malmkjær 2020: 73).

The licence-taking unleashed by modernism eventually reached publications of noted experimentality such as the Zukofskys' homophonic *Catullus* (1969): suiting the sound-sense of the Latin originals on English phrasing and taking an inclination of modernist translation to prioritize and amplify an aspect of form and of reader's experience to an extreme. Decades later, Catullus is subject to a more granular treatment at the hands of Anne Carson as she pays prismatic attention to a single Catullan ode, illuminating functions of commemoration and elegy in the ways the self is both veiled and revealed through a staged translating of classical text. *Nox* (2010) finds her recording and modulating a process that turns autobiographical as a deceased brother is gradually discovered via consequent drafts and translation research: Latin to English as a scaffolding for the telling of grief.

Classical versioning, as understood in this Element, is often a close relative of recontextualization: in excerpting from the original and effecting juxtapositions with a modern consciousness, or conversing with a body of work, where the classical intertext is simultaneously revealed to be a hidden core. It is not surprising that the many terms describing insertion of subjectivity are promoted to book titles: Lowell's *Imitations*, already mentioned; in Derek Mahon's *The Adaptations 1975–2020* (2022), we cannot fail to notice how choruses and passages from Sophocles, Aristophanes, Lucretius, Sextus Propertius, Ovid, and Juvenal take up almost the first 50 pages of a nearly 200-page volume that progresses to dozens more authors, all the way to Michel Houellebecq. For someone like Tony Harrison, the presence of classical past into tumultuous present guides their process and drives their work. He comments on his version of *Hecuba* thus:

> In my notebooks, where I glue pictures among the drafts of translations from the Greek tragedies I've adapted for the stage, is the recurring image of an old woman appealing to the camera that has captured her agony, or to the heavens that ignore it, in front of a devastated home or before her murdered dead. They are all different women from many places on earth with the same gesture of disbelief, despair and denunciation. They are in Sarajevo, Kosovo, Grozny, Gaza, Ramallah, Tbilisi, Baghdad, Falluja – women in robes and men in metal helmets as in the Trojan war. Under them all, over the years, I have scribbled 'Hecuba'. My notebooks are bursting with Hecubas. Hecuba walks out of Euripides from 2,500 years ago straight on to our daily front pages and into our nightly newscasts. To our shame she is news that stays news. (Harrison 2005)

Theatrical space returns these realities to the classical original via creative reconfigurations that contain a strong political and activist component. And taking a cue from the glued pictures on Harrison's notebook, a recontextualization assisted by images also interests us: creative classical translation is reflected in how the verbal and the visual conspire in accelerating our recognition of analogies in different time frames. In *Still* (2016), thirty poem-versions drawn from Virgil's *Georgics* by Simon Armitage are provoked by and accompany twenty-six century-old photos from the Battle of the Somme. The result is a joint comment on the movements and devastation of war on the European landscape.

The language one embarks from is a further demarcating line: it may or may not be the original one in versioning, while the question is more settled (or expected to be) when we speak of translation. With Pound, we encounter either scenario; poet-translators like Carson and Balmer are classicists with an intimate knowledge of ancient Greek or Latin; they abstract from and metabolize something that *could have been* a translation. On the other hand, Hughes' lack of access to the languages of classical antiquity – and consequently his reliance on literals for such work – was reflected upon as creative direction. Scholars have pointed out how Hughes embraced something akin to Walter Benjamin's 'pure' language, admiring 'the immediacy, the spontaneity, the almost folk-quality of the rough, unfinished, midway translated text ...', owned by everyone and by no one' (Bergin 2018: 79). Redirecting the economies and aesthetic of the literal inside the process results in a more immediate, ascetic language and a product that could be described as 'a poetically reinforced impression' of the English literals. Functional English cribs that were supposed to merely aid translation became the texts Hughes strived to imitate. An entire *oeuvre* manifests an effort to reduce expression to what felt essential.

Also achieved through this manner is a relocation of images, modes, and ideas, occasionally seen in notes or in letters – for instance, when Hughes devises a new ending for *Seneca's Oedipus* (1969) that involves a giant 'serpent penis 30 feet long & full of people' (letter to Peter Redgrove, quoted in Rees 2018: 127). While the idea was never realized for the stage, it is later transfused into 'Oedipus Crow' and 'Song for a Phallus' (Hughes 1972: 35 and 69–71 respectively). The poetic register, triggered by Seneca, spills over to most of the material in that seminal collection. Hughes' letter to Nick Gammage in 1992 is equally of import ('Yes, I translated Seneca's Oedipus in among writing the Crow pieces ... Main influence was – the stylistic release of finding a simple language and tone for a supercharged theme ... Affected the style of Crow'; Rees 2018: 127) in confirming essential ways in which the writing of originals and classical translation pollinate each other. As Trinacty (2016: 479–505) has shown, there is hardly a point where intertextuality is not part of the picture;

intertexts in such translations may mark translations as instances of metapoetic, thematic, and philosophical reflection – and in the case of poets like Hughes, they become sites in which the reception of predecessors is negotiated:

> Even in a translation that attempts to be concise to the point of severely simplifying the language, *we can see the importance of intertextuality and reception. Hughes, like Seneca and Ovid before him, cannot separate himself from the time in which he lives and the strong influence of the poetry on which he was raised* (Shakespeare, Yeats, Housman). Hughes's echoes of these poets provide startling and evocative insight to his view of the Oedipus legend or Ovid's creation, *by allowing these later poets to answer questions posed in the original . . . or to accentuate the atmosphere and themes found therein.* (p. 502; my emphases)

A final example of this sort of empathy or possession comes courtesy of the *Dionysiaca* of Nonnus, a 2022 'group translation' that we shall return to in Section 4. Carson comments on her own translating of Book 23 that it would be helpful to know 'how devout Nonnus was and when that started. It would be helpful to know if he had a sense of humor' ('On Translating Nonnus' 2022: 731). She continues: 'I couldn't help a sort of high-styled archness pervading the language of my translation and am still not sure whether this came more from me or from him' (pp. 731–2). She tellingly concludes by mentioning the existence of 'a few locutions I didn't find a way to use' (p. 732). Remainders from the process that already resulted in a published portion from an ancient epic, these locutions are sequenced and appended to Carson's (statement on the) translation. 'Together', Carson speculates, 'they almost make what in Icelandic is called a *drápustúfr* ("poem stump").

> Abrim,
> oversalted,
> transpicuous,
> big knotty penis
> and gold all up your grill.
> What would the fox say?'
>
> ('On Translating Nonnus' 2022: 732)

2 Conductors of Homer

Hearers and Readers

Prevalent as our attention may be towards the *Iliad* and the *Odyssey*, a discussion of Homeric translation should include reminders of material beyond these two epics: a number of hymns were also attributed to Homer in antiquity. The opening paragraph of Athanassakis' preface to his translation of

The Homeric Hymns (1976) is illustrative of a sense of responsibility to a lesser-known classical source text:

> Poetry is untranslatable, and the present translation does not claim to be poetry. My rendition is a line-by-line English version of the original Greek. I have aimed for accuracy rather than for poetic effect, although, wherever I could, I tried to preserve for the reader the vigor and beauty of the original. I did not modernize traditional renditions of certain epithets and phrases, and I refused to lengthen or truncate lines for metrical or symmetrical purposes. I made an effort to keep to an iambic flow, but here again I preferred to violate this flow rather than to sacrifice accuracy. The reason for a verse translation rather than a prose translation is simple: the reader can refer to lines more easily, and should he be interested in comparing this rendition with the Greek text, he will find it easier to do so. In addition to this, a straight prose translation would bear even less resemblance to the original. (Athanassakis 1976: viii)

Stern and inflexible, Athanassakis shows us how anxieties about fidelity may trump everything else: his is a baseline of actions for conveying these hymns with *accuracy* to a modern reader. This model barely allows the idea of translation to enter the frame – we are given a 'line-by-line version'. And staying with verse owes more to practical purposes of comparison, to a proximity with the original form, than any debts to poetry. Modernizing is also out of the question: rather, the original must be salvaged, any admixtures in process or product guarded against. Athanassakis desires totality of closeness and offers us translation-as-document. And yet, individual hymns have certainly been approached otherwise before: there is, for instance, a spirited version of the 'Hymn to Mercury' by Shelley (1820).

Even when a freer path is taken, there are gradations to it. Introducing the text of his radio drama of the *Odyssey* (2006), Armitage feels that any *Odyssey* will inevitably 'ring with echoes and resonances of our contemporary world' and therefore sees no need to depict Achaeans 'as veterans of the Gulf War or asylum-seekers' (Armitage 2008: vi). No anachronisms are required, yet lines are crossed *and* Armitage produces a radio play which he hoped 'should have further life as a piece of writing' (p. vi). Intended for BBC Radio 4, this *Odyssey* is geared towards listeners and displays a poet's ear for phrasing and rhythm; the cover of the 2008 American edition even defines it as 'a dramatic retelling', yet another term for the creativity the reader must be made aware of. Athanassakis and Armitage present two points on a spectrum; what *any* approach to Homer must confront, however, is the question of authorship, more consequential here than in perhaps any other case of a classical author. Athanassakis reminds us of ascription to ancient poets – also called the *Homeridae* – for some of the hymns, and about the instability that characterizes the texts we have – in the case of the

Hymns, collated from more than thirty-one manuscripts scattered across Europe (see Athanassakis 1976: x). Homer remains a ghostly figure even in the ancient past: biographies by archaic Greeks are understood to be fictitious, either based on inferences from the Homeric poems themselves or little more than pure invention. Uncertainties surrounding the author and text are themselves a source of translational creativity, and few have made the point better than Borges (1999: 70) in 'The Homeric Versions':

> That heterogenous and even contradictory richness is not attributable solely to the evolution of the English language, or to the mere length of the original, or to the deviations or diverse capacities of the translators, but rather to a circumstance that is particular to Homer: the difficult category of knowing what pertains to the poet and what pertains to the language. To that fortunate difficulty we owe the possibility of so many versions, all of them sincere, genuine, and divergent.

Realizations of an impossible fidelity also spur re-imaginings. Homer's biography can be extended, re-visioned. Today, the epics can be read through the lens of gender studies, or class issues, or postcolonial writing, and filled with potencies of identity. With the ancient author blurred, other subjectivities, including that of the translator, creatively intrude. This may inflect our reading of translations new and old; versioning is more welcome in this context, and arguably the space is created from which a wealth of allusive potentials may emerge, from *Batrachomyomachia*, that ancient parody of the *Iliad*, to the Homeric references populating Byron's *Don Juan* (1819–24); then there is Kazantzakis' *Odyssey: A Modern Sequel* (1938), totalling 33,333 lines; Glück's repurposing of Homer as comment on a relationship within *Meadowlands* (1996); the partial reimagining of Books 22–4 of the *Iliad* that is Malouf's *Ransom* (2009); Atwood's restoring of agency to the wife of Odysseus in *The Penelopiad* (2005); the recentring of the *Iliad* in Barker's *The Silence of the Girls* (2017), from the wrath of Achilles to the plight of Briseis and women like her; and a similar installing of modern consciousness concerned with gender reaches us at points in Stoppard's dramatic monologue *Penelope* (2022), designed for 'two voices, a singer and an actor, both of them Penelope' (Stoppard 2022: vii).

These are all readers of Homer – and of Homer in translation, more often than not. Few examples have been more emblematic than Keats' sonnet 'On First Looking into Chapman's Homer' (1816). Webb (2004: 304) ably describes a web of interrelations when he argues that what Keats appears to commemorate and celebrate in that poem

> is a recognition both of Homer and of Chapman, or rather of Homer through Chapman. For once, translator and the object of translation (or in technical

terms, the target text) are intimately and indissolubly connected. The poem pays homage to Homer but the memory it recreates is of hearing 'Chapman speak out loud and bold', an experience which provides the poet with access to a new level of literary consciousness. The title reminds Keats' readers that this is a poem about reading but the final line of the octet insists on the oral, or the aural.

Translation theorists are even more cognizant of how we experience the classics as a palimpsest of previous readings. Bassnett (2019: 96–102) follows inscriptions on a copy of Lattimore's 1951 translation, entrusted to her by a bookseller: the previous owner was Sylvia Plath. Bassnett's perusing of this annotated *Iliad* engenders reflection on how Homer may lead to further literary art, as happens with Logue's *War Music* or Longley's Iliadic allusion in 'Ceasefire' (1994), a poem that recalls Priam's pleading stance towards Achilles, published only days after the Provisional IRA announced a truce. Bassnett is reminded of her own formative experiences with (Italian) translations of the *Iliad* at a young age and the fact that she used to skip over the violent descriptive passages. At the same time, as she reads Plath's copy in an age when conflicts are constantly tracked on the television news, it appears that 'human beings are as cruel and callous in war as Homer described them in the eighth century BC' (Bassnett 2019: 99).

An Anglo-American Series

The numerous versions of the *Odyssey* in English literature, Borges (1999: 70) assures us, 'would be enough to illustrate the course of its centuries'. Early on especially, scenes and characters move freely between genres and languages; Wilson (2004: 275) reminds us that '"Homer" before the eighteenth-century colonization of the classics was a more composite and more uncertain entity. Troy was Homer's terrain, and a magnet for local "Homeric" emotion both for visitors and in the imagination, but Troy in European and English literature is not always or even primarily Homeric.' Aspects of the *Iliad*'s plot were especially familiar to readers before the first (and partial) translation of the first ten books, published by Hall in 1581. There was Lydgate's *Troy Book*, an account of legends from the Trojan War completed in 1420 for Henry V, and eventually published in 1513 to join the very popular *Recuyell of the Histories of Troye* from Caxton (1474). Both influenced generations of poets, but they are mediated through varied sources, these often being plain invention by medieval poets, accumulating towards what we now generally call the 'Matter of Troy'. Instead of translating the *Iliad*, many of the successive iterations in European languages originated in the third and fifth centuries AD and from Latin renderings of the supposed 'eye-witness' memoirs of the Trojan War by 'Dictys the

Cretan' and 'Dares the Phrygian'. Each arrived with adjustments in form and storyline. Similarly, Chaucer's *Troilus and Criseyde* (1383) borrows heavily from *Il Filostrato* (1340) and the Italian of Boccaccio – yet also conceives and adds a source (the non-existent Lollius). The fact that Troilus is barely mentioned in Homer, and Cressida is altogether absent from the *Iliad*, is telling of the amalgamations taking place.

Homer and Troy were thus told and retold in England for centuries before we truly come to translation; when this occurs with Chapman, a cycle of inspirations develops anew even as his *Iliad*, completed in 1615, finds classical translation still triangulating sources rather than directly engaging the classical original. Chapman may have relied on the Greek text compiled by Spondanus, but in that edition a parallel Latin translation by Andreas Divus faced the Greek text. Underwood (1998: 20) points out that the Latin appears to have formed the basis for Chapman's translation, and 'Chapman also used a wide range of secondary sources, such as lexicons, commentaries, and versions of the original in Latin, Italian, or French. Even his Greek dictionary, Scapula's lexicon of 1580, was Greek to Latin rather than Greek to English.' We can trace the Latinisms permeating this 'fourteener' Homer, and Chapman's overt enthusing about etymology, to these sources. Translation may be second-hand yet it is explained as a product of affinity in the comments around the text. The metaphors used and ornamentations in phrasing are reflective of Elizabethan poetics, and Chapman's frequent installations of compound word forms squeezed further Homer's language and epithets. As a result, many readers encountered a complexity that made it hard to follow Chapman's – or Homer's – thought. Yet Coleridge defends the work on the basis of poetry in a letter to Wordsworth quoted by Hooper in his introduction to a later *Iliad*, that of Alexander Pope:

> Chapman writes & feels as a Poet – as Homer might have written had he lived in England in the reign of Queen Elizabeth – in short, it is an exquisite poem, in spite of its frequent & perverse quaintnesses & harshnesses, which are however amply repaid by almost unexampled sweetness & beauty of language, all over spirit & feeling. In the main it is an English Heroic Poem, the tale of which is borrowed from the Greek. (Hooper 1888: xvii)

Only a few noteworthy versions were completed in the century that intervened between Chapman's translation and that of Pope, completed between 1715 and 1720. Pope equally draws on previous translations and alludes to Milton, Virgil, and Dryden. This Homer has significance as an action to consolidate the reputation Pope had already achieved as a poet, but also a position implied, with regards to what was then known as 'the Quarrel'.

Originating in French intellectual circles in the seventeenth century, a progressive faction (the 'Moderns') sought to rid Renaissance Europe of allegiance to the classical past, while the 'Ancients' were invested in the study of predecessors and saw antiquity as integral to the literary creation that might follow. Translation, its practices, and choices involved in it are bound to enter the picture: so it is with Pope, who essentially translates in a context where the manners of both gods and heroes were vulnerable 'to the proprieties of seventeenth-century neo-classicism and religion. Travesty and burlesque abound in English responses to Homer and translations of Homer' (Wilson 2004: 276).

Through his heroic couplets, Pope also joins Homer with the poetry of the time and we can begin to trace, with Brower, how theories of literature and attitudes to translation coalesce: '[t]he notion of "the true heroick poem" – to us, one of the curiosities of literature – seemed to the literary public of the seventeenth and eighteenth centuries exactly as valid as the theory of traditional oral composition seems to present-day writers on the epic' (Brower 1974: 66). Steiner (2004: 367) argues that it is a conception of Homer as 'the ultimate master of poetic invention' that induces Pope 'to attenuate, even to elide what he judges to be gross or primitive in Homeric theology and in certain episodes of the war at Troy. In counterpart, Pope amplifies and elaborates on what he feels to be the pictorial elements in Homer's aesthetics, as well as on the morally sententious.' (The thread of visual art allowing us to access or make analogies with a preliterate text continues to this day, variously reflected in, for instance, Logue's drawing on ideas from cinema or the fluidity and abstractions of William Tillyer's watercolours that accompany Oswald's *Odyssey* variations in *Nobody: A Hymn to the Sea* (2021).[2]) But it all begins with union felt with the original author: 'Homer secretly seems inclined to a correspondence with me, in letting me into a good part of his intentions' (Pope's letter to Joseph Addison, 30 January 1713–14; see Pope 1956: 208). Nor will writing and translating be kept separate, as we often observe in similar cases. *The Rape of the Lock* (1712) – which doubles as a parody of the *Iliad* – incorporates ideas from Pope's then translation-in-progress. These are pervasively intertwined works.

We can speak of Homeric reception 'after Pope'. Further attempts visibly or implicitly to respond to Pope include Cowper's translations of the two epics, emerging in 1791 from an aversion to what he felt were Pope's inaccuracies; but it only serves to show that a Homer in English is now worth pursuing, and translation thought follows the matter closely, not least when Arnold, reacting to

---

[2] Tillyer's work originating in this collaboration with Oswald was exhibited at the Bernard Jacobson Gallery between 26 April and 23 June 2018. For details, see: www.jacobsongallery.com/exhib itions/33-william-tillyer-and-alice-oswald-nobody/.

earlier excesses, lays out criteria for the *Iliad* in his 1861 lectures 'On Translating Homer'.

The twentieth century saw a quickening of translation. Retranslation in this sense is a phenomenon of note. Steiner has also conveyed the sense in which the exilic experiences and displacement of modernity turn us towards the *Odyssey*, while the constancy of conflict, from two world wars to Vietnam and beyond, reaches for explanation and reflection in multiplications of the *Iliad* (see esp. Steiner 1996: 100; 2004: 372). Later studies confirm this tendency, among them Vandiver (2010) which examines a range of classical receptions in the context of dealing with the trauma of the First World War. While tensions between scholarly and literary ideals of translation remain, an enlarged array of responses emerges in the twentieth century, and not merely drawing on the translations that have come before. Throughout modernity, posits Steiner (2004: 372; my emphasis), the dialogue of Homeric translation and poetry becomes inescapable, with new renderings sourcing equally creative retellings: texts 'such as Auden's "Shield of Achilles", Ezra Pound's *Cantos* or Joyce's *Ulysses* greatly influence, be it subliminally, both readers *and translators* of the Iliad and the Odyssey'. Milieus of reading also affected how Homeric translation was approached. Rieu's prose renderings of the *Odyssey* (1946) and *Iliad* (1950) are inextricably linked to an outlook of 'easy reading for those who are unfamiliar with the Greek world' (Homer 1946: i) – the 1946 *Odyssey* being the inaugural title of Penguin Classics: and so a generation of readers will have experienced Homer through Rieu's novelistic shapes. The preface foreshadows the path taken and links the original with readers' experience in the present: 'the *Odyssey*, with its well-knit plot, its psychological interest and its interplay of character, is the true ancestor of the long line of novels which have followed it' (p. viii).

Lattimore's *Iliad* again manifests a Homer read through preceding translations. Writing for *The Kenyon Review*, Fitzgerald (1952: 698–706) registers how Lattimore 'brings Homer back from the prose where he has been getting submerged for the past several generations and restores him to his proper element, which is poetry and magnificence' (p. 699). More importantly, the reconnection with poetry entails that for at least two generations

> verse has been appropriating some of the rhythms of prose. Hopkins' sprung rhythm, concentrated on the beat with outriding syllables, was a manner of appropriation; Pound's style of suspended cadences and parenthetical rhymes was another; and Eliot has supplied some particularly spidery and distinguished examples. William Carlos Williams – the extreme case – has never written a poem in regular meter and apparently has no ear for it. I have called this development an appropriation, meaning to imply that poetry has gained

by it rather than lost. It has enabled Lattimore to give us this *Iliad*, and will enable a great many readers to get through it, thereby experiencing something they will not encounter elsewhere in literature: the immense swell and fall of the heroic poem. (pp. 701–2)

A 2012 round-up review of new translations and recastings of the epics of Homer points us, through Mitchell's (Homer 2011) contentious decision to remove Book 10 (on account of D. L. West's edition of the *Iliad* and his perspectives on the *Doloneia* especially as an addition by a different poet; Homerus and West 1998; West 2011), to the philological limits detected on the translator, here clearly felt to have exceeded their mandate:

> I suspect I will not be the only reader to be annoyed by having my mind made up for me in advance by the translator, especially when the ongoing debate remains so hard-fought. Surely the translator's business is to use the traditional text without excisions (though with a warning about the doubts expressed in antiquity regarding Book Ten), and let the reader make up his or her own mind. (Green 2012)

In statements surrounding her translation of Homer, Wilson (2019: 295) notes how even the 1996 Fagles translation, celebrated at the time of publication for bringing psychological subtlety to rendering the women in the *Odyssey*, is pursuant of a host of assumptions about heteronormative institutions, at points sentimentalizing marriage and also ignoring 'the huge inequality of economic and social power in this idealized relationship ... Penelope's choices operate within an extremely circumscribed arena'. Accounts of the 1996 translation by Fagles himself in its paratexts, or by reviewers at the time, 'as "politically correct" or even "feminist" could be read as a measure of how far gender awareness has come in the past twenty years' (ibid.: 296). Similar attitudes define the 'Translator's Note' to her *Odyssey* (Wilson 2018: 81–91), which equally illustrates how far classical translators have come in being aware of a creative and critical horizon. Wilson reminds us how embedded some issues are in theorizations of literary translation: 'The gendered metaphor of the "faithful" translation, whose worth is always secondary to that of a male-authored original, acquires a particular edge in the context of a translation by a woman of *The Odyssey*, a poem that is deeply invested in female fidelity and male dominance' (p. 86). Wilson next translates *The Iliad* (Homer 2023), a project entailing further opportunities to investigate the translator's agency.

Forms of Delivery

A concern with accessibility has continued at least since Rieu's translation and has motivated Homeric re-creations from the mid-twentieth century to the present. We recognize it in the prose tendencies of Robert Graves, as he searches in *The Anger of Achilles* for forms that will rescue the epic from the 'classroom curse'. His retelling proceeds from the realization that, in the wake of the printing press, novels and histories in the West at least 'need no longer be clothed in regular metre to make them easily memorized; nor do English versions of the *Iliad*. Broken meter, which some recent translators adopt, seems to me an unfortunate compromise between verse and prose' (Graves 1959: 34–5). And Graves claims simply to be following the example of the ancient Irish and Welsh bards by 'taking up my harp and singing only where prose will not suffice. This, I hope, avoids the pitfalls of either an all-prose or an all-verse translation, and restores something of the *Iliad*'s value as mixed entertainment' (p. 35).

Although 'all-verse', Logue's *War Music*, straddling the twentieth and twenty-first centuries, is worlds apart from the translations that trouble Graves and manifests a plethora of modernism-guided responses to the epic. 'What Logue took to heart so effectively', Bainbridge (2005) points out, 'were Pound's technical innovations, his cinematic evocation of place and landscape, his sensitivity to typography, his use of imagery and rhythm. The essence of Logue's achievement has been to combine these features with an exhilarating narrative drive and a remarkable sensitivity to the energies of contemporary language.' *War Music* began as a radio version of rhapsody 16, published eventually as *Patrocleia* in 1962. Thirty years later, and fifteen years before the last volume appeared during Logue's lifetime (2005's *Cold Calls: War Music continued*, which is the subject of Bainbridge's (2005) review), the modern poet reminds us of the significance of voice in the introduction to *Kings* (Logue 1991) and succinctly explains a creative remit in which he 'concocted a storyline' that was based on material in this early part of Homer's poem, to which he 'added a scene or two of my own, and then, knowing no Greek but having got from the translations made in the accepted sense of the word the gist of what this or that character said, attempted to make their voices come alive, and to keep the action on the move' (p. ix).

Far more is being attempted than Logue suggests. Fragments of other war literature, key utterances sourced from critical moments in world civilization, are embedded in volumes such as *The Husbands* (1994) and beyond. Underwood discussed these insertions of post-Homeric references as anachronisms or 'time travelling collage' in his 1998 volume on *English Translators of Homer*, which ends with Logue, although when *Cold Calls* is later examined, he concurs with Taplin's (2007) point that Logue's Homer 'straddles different time zones, without being fixed in a specific time, so the concept of anachronism does not apply' (Underwood 2014: 90) and thus 'time tension(s)' is a more effective term for what is taking place. As I have argued in a previous discussion of *War Music* (Nikolaou 2017: 17–40), Pound's definition of the epic as a 'poem including history' is paralleled by Logue's own 'translation including history', where we often encounter

> autobiographical texts: lines from memoirs, and reported voices that are 'there' and appear to observe and relate to us a diversity of conflict settings. The poet thus injects splinters of subjectivity – together, inevitably, with their respective historical moments – from the seventeenth century battlefield of Edgehill and the trenches of the First World War, to the slums of Harlem. Those para-sites append themselves to the body of Logue's account; participatory echoes, expert witnesses.
>
> Perhaps more urgently than in original writing, intertextual elements within poetic translation point to autographic imperatives of a reading consciousness. (Nikolaou 2017: 31–2)

The notes appended to the end of Logue's volumes list these references – many of them snapshots of his own reading of Homer; and the constant renaming of translation, moreover, is itself part of the discourse of creativity when it comes to (classical) translation. *All Day Permanent Red* (2003) being subtitled 'the first battle scenes of Homer's *Iliad* rewritten' is an example.

We also glimpse Homer in Balmer's work, versioned and recontextualized inside modern experience. In *Chasing Catullus: Poems, Translations and Transgressions* (2004), where classical allusion is deployed in responding to the death of Balmer's niece from cancer, the third section ('After') is fronted by a fragment from the *Aeneid* and comprises fifteen poems, the first three under the title 'Heroics'. A 'condensed' Book 22 of the *Iliad* starts things off, and Balmer's notes at the end of the book are suggestive of what may be envisioned through creative classical translation. We learn that her reworking of *Iliad* Book 22 as 'Fresh Meat' was

> commissioned by the journal *perversions* . . . The poem plays on the Greek's homoerotic sub-text, not just of Achilles' love for Patroclus but also the subconscious undercurrent of desire between the two opposing warriors, particularly in a speech by Hector . . . I perverted my version with this reading, changing the distant, third-person narrative of Homer's epic into the first person lament of Hector's ghost. (Balmer 2004a: 62)

It is also a reminder of how notes and critical commentary can illuminate and enhance the poet-translator's intent. In the sequence of twelve *Odyssey*-inspired poems coming after 'Heroics' (Balmer 2004a: 46–57), the notes again help us register how the meanings of Homeric scenes and analogies transpiring in British or Irish landscapes are woven together: 'II. Glendalough' connects the ancient Irish monastic site to the Cyclops episode; the note for 'Chapel Downs' similarly informs us of the ancient Celtic site of the title, and the italic passage that is embedded in Balmer's poem (one of many such instances across the collection) is one 'translated from *Odyssey*, 10.194–97' (where Odysseus and his men encounter Circe on the island of Aeaea); 'Letchworth Crematorium' reworks *Odyssey* 11.24–43 and, along with poems V–VIII from the sequence, is based on the rhapsody describing the hero's decent into the Underworld (known as *Nekyia*, or 'Book of the Dead'). Balmer even blends elements from later poetic allusions to Homer – as evidenced from the title of 'X. Return to Ithaca (VIA CAVAFY)'.

In *Letting Go*, from 2017, including poems written following the sudden death of Balmer's mother, we find, among a few Homeric incursions, the epic simile in Book 12 of the *Iliad* comparing the missiles of the Greeks to snow falling across Troy 'Veiling the forest hills, dark, distant Downs, / Levelling fresh ploughed farmland' (p. 19). The simile that described a siege millennia ago now reaches an English church where a funeral is going to take place, and the snow 'pales the priest's black coat as he clears paths' (p. 19). Such assured closing of distances through poetic reconstitutions of Homeric material also describes imperatives of versioning and the paratextual plan of many an *Iliad* or *Odyssey* in English, as seen in this section. A Troy of always is often sought via translational, critical, and re-creative equivalents of cinema's 'jump-cut'.

Orality As Creativity

An imagining of preliterate environments often spurs creativity in Homeric translation – its processes and products engaging the oral transitioning into writing, stylized into text. Relations between performance, orality, and translational creativity are therefore especially active, and a cursory look at paratexts shows that translators and editors alike are keen to regulate the experience of readers: in her introduction to Lombardo's translation of the *Iliad* (Homer 1997), Sheila Murnaghan argues that his

> version highlights the living connection that the poet builds between himself and his audience and his evocation of the spontaneous and idiosyncratic accents of the individual speakers whom he impersonates. In doing so, Lombardo brings out yet another way in which the concerns of the poet intersect with those of his characters, for in his recreation of heroic warfare, Homer has made it a realm not only of forceful action, but also of powerful speaking. (Murnaghan 1997: lviii)

It belongs in a long line of similar attitudes. Pope recognized the special power and presence of the speeches in the *Iliad* in his own preface and further sought to enhance the sense of oratory across the epic. Staying with merely two, yet radically different, approaches to Homer in English, the one by Lombardo vis-à-vis the elliptical collision of genres that defines Oswald's *Memorial* from 2011 should enable us to better sense how an orality recaptured is among the constants for a Homer given to today's readers. Lombardo remains perhaps the translator most conscientiously incorporating performance in both the development of a translation and how its results are transmitted. A desire to find the voice behind the text appears to be shaped by his own Zen practice – another instance of classical translation that turns individualized, its creativity also located at the level of process and even more so in terms of the translator's autobiography and life choices existing in dialogue with the work of the ancient author. Lombardo offers details in a paper titled 'Homer's Light: The Odyssey Koan' (Lombardo 2001) but also more recently, in interview responses, where he again stresses that the

> point was about really grasping the other person's mind in what's felt as a direct way – and only then, the language follows. It's been a paradigm for me for a long time. After all, I began Zen practice in the mid-70s, nearly about when I started to translate. It has been a parallel development, almost. [3]

Performing the translation in progress is an integral part of engaging the text for this translator of Homer and, indeed, forms it decisively.

Classical translation is also impelled and inspired by previous responses – some of them experienced, for good reason, as originals. As reader, Lombardo contends that Logue

> gets at something essential in Homer in *Patrocleia*; he's certainly not staying close to the language, and very often ... he will have asides. But for me there's something just intrinsically Homeric about what he's doing ... I can put it this way: reading Book 16 in Greek, and I've certainly done that many times – and actually performed it, so I'm very, very familiar with the text and have been for a long time – and listening to Christopher Logue read out loud, Logue *in performance*: I don't even want to call it a similarity, but there's some kind of *consonance*. Something really essential. One's hair stands up – in the same way as when I read Homer. I understand *and have the same emotional connection with the two pieces*. [4]

Beyond the overall modernist logic of Logue's versioning, this is a Homer crucially shaped early on by the performance poetry and combinations of poetry and jazz that served Logue's political and protest poems of the early 1960s. Even some of the typographical experiments in *Patrocleia* can be traced to his poster poems from that period. These are all elements that combine to assist the

---

[3] Drawing from an interview with Stanley Lombardo and the author conducted in April 2021.
[4] Ibid., my emphases.

poem being *heard* by the reader, with scholars like Greenwood (2009: 506) arguing that in many respects 'sense follows sound throughout' Logue's engagement with Homer. It is a perspective Lombardo appears to echo when stating that 'Logue's is real poetry in the sense that Homer is real poetry, and it is intended to be performed', something that does not occur to him 'when I teach Fitzgerald or many of the other translators'.[5] This reaction to an early part of *War Music* is suggestive not only of the sense of energy retained and redirected when we read certain versions but also of how voice and performance communicate such achievement. Lombardo also attaches such a requirement to more proper translations of Homer ('consequently in my case also, I did not feel that my publication of the *Iliad* and the *Odyssey* was complete, until I recorded the audio books; then it's truly been made public').[6] In a broader sense, the rise of platforms like Audible arguably help key us once more into oral transmission, themselves a shaping factor in how the translated, classical text-to-be-read is crafted and managed.

After-images of this orality are pursued in another drastic reorganization of Iliadic material; the opening paragraph of an essay by Georgina Paul, on Oswald's *Memorial* and Barbara Köhler's *Niemands Frau* (Nobody's Wife, 2007), finds the researcher transmitting a powerful impression made on her by Oswald reading the work:[7]

> On 12 November 2012 I went to the Ioannou Centre in the University of Oxford to hear what I thought was going to be a reading by the British poet Alice Oswald of her poem *Memorial*. But Alice Oswald didn't read; she recited from memory. For the hour and twenty minutes that it takes to recite the entire poem, the audience in the lecture theatre watched and listened to the poet standing with raised head and steady gaze, never looking down to refer to a text, while from her lips the words flowed and flowed and flowed as if they had never had anything to do with writing: terrible words telling of violent deaths, words which penetrated the body, making it identify with the ravages described, making the listener self-conscious about the vulnerability of teeth and skulls and flesh, yet that violence interspersed with passages of ethereally beautiful lyric. That recital taught me why the ancients believed poetic speech to be inspired by a divine entity. The words seemed God's words, the poet a messenger from another place. (Paul 2019: 143)

There are echoes here of Lombardo listening to Logue in performance. And Oswald further pursues how imaginings of orality may reside again in our written spaces with 'Tithonus' (see Oswald 2016: 45–81), another fable

---

[5] Ibid. [6] Ibid.
[7] Key excerpts from the audio CD recording of *Memorial* (2011) can be found at The Poetry Archive website: https://poetryarchive.org/poem/memorial/ and https://poetryarchive.org/poem/memorial-part-2/.

drawn from Homer where a comparable mode of textual iconicity operates, here including layout and typography to emphasize the coexistence of a durational performance.

Creativity that partakes in choices involved in actual performances of translated classics, similarly to resourceful editing, can direct the reader towards making auxiliary connections: throwing light onto intertexts, the influences shared by ancient authors, or key junctures between Greek and Roman traditions. In one such example, Lombardo tells us about combining passages from the *Iliad* and a later, unfinished epic by Statius, revolving around the childhood of the Greek hero:

> I've done performances of those passages both in the *Iliad* and the *Achilleid*, between Achilles and his mother, where they interact in some kind of way . . . So, in the *Iliad*, it's when she brings him the armour the one she forged for him in Book 19, and it ends there. The end of the *Achilleid* is when the ship that's taking him to Troy lands there; maybe 100 lines into the second book. That's as far as [Statius] got. And so I have that also included in the performance – even though his mother is not a part of that – but to tie them together . . . The *Achilleid* presents a unique balance of very strong Greek and Latin influences, epic influences. And the way the poem ends . . . it just takes you right back into the *Iliad*, where it all starts. It's a beautiful circle. [8]

The 'beautiful circle' that Lombardo recognizes also describes several of the diverse, modern(ist) reconnections to the experience of a preliterate culture and the ways in which contemporary translations and versions of Homer seek to embed in their textual constitutions the transition to, and subsequent layers of, writing, all the while eliciting and enacting the fluidity and impermanence of the oral and the aural that once inspired a sonnet by Keats to a translation of Homer.

3 American Arrangements
The Classical and the Political

When Peter Green defends 'Lattimore's program' as one that included 'meter, rhythm, style, formulaic phrases, vocabulary, and those qualities famously isolated by Matthew Arnold in his lectures *On Translating Homer*: rapidity, plainness of thought, directness of expression, and a nobility of concept that could rise, without losing its simplicity, to the grand manner', he also immediately makes the connection that '[t]he occasion that produced such an English *Iliad* was, of course, the huge expansion of American university education in the humanities, largely fostered by the GI Bill in the years immediately following World War II' (Green 2012). Broader dimensions of

---

[8] Quoted from the earlier-mentioned April 2021 interview with Lombardo.

classical reception, distinctive references, and emphases were cultivated as peoples across the new world gradually formed national identities. Here, the written word is one facet of many: American architecture has long been preoccupied with neoclassical features. Arguably, a need for continuity and projection of shared tradition and values appears more acute in US cities, not least considering the short time frame in which these were built, compared with urban centres in Europe.

Certain themes or characters allow for scenes of recognition or present opportunities for subversion. Roynon (2021) shows how copiously and diversely classical texts have been dwelled upon, from Willa Cather's engagement with classical mythology and texts in her poetry, prose, and non-fiction, to reflections on the nature of tragedy across Philip Roth's *The Human Stain* (2000), to the intertwining of Christian belief and classical myth that takes place in Marilynne Robinson's *Gilead* (2004). The novelists studied by Roynon (2021: 34) deploy 'classical culture to construct specific versions of individual racial, socio-economic and/or gendered identities and experiences' at key moments in the history of the United States. She presses the point by arguing that in books like Ralph Ellison's posthumous *Three Days before the Shooting* ... (2010), or the figure of Prometheus in Roth's *I Married a Communist* (1998), classical allusions 'are never merely an aesthetic phenomenon. They are always ideological in effect, playing a central role in a novel's interactions with the historical, political and cultural contexts which it is shaped by and which it shapes' (Roynon 2021: 34). Identifications are prolific. Ellison's *Invisible Man* (1952), for instance, deploys the Cyclops figure to thematize ways of seeing or being blind to post-war American racism, as McConnell (2013) points out, in a study that presciently discusses several key postcolonial literary projects that also use elements from the *Odyssey* as mainframe and counterpoint.

Nor can we afford to overlook comics, a genre quintessentially American in its origin, and those abundant classical presences therein: from superheroes' analogous function to that of ancient mythological figures to more mature examples in the form of graphic novels like Mazzuchelli's *Asterios Polyp* (2009), which is permeated with classical allusions (more notably as the protagonist, a 'paper architect', identifies with both Odysseus and Orpheus), to the urgency of intentions and more systematic imposition of epic plotline in Duggan and Noto's *The Infinite Horizon* (2012), a reconfiguration of the *Odyssey* that reflects on post-9/11 foreign policy and the geopolitical upheaval resulting from the Iraq War through a soldier's return home. And perhaps we come full circle to illuminating, through the genre, workings of translation and adaptation in *The Trojan Women: A Comic* (2021), where a version of Euripides by Carson fuses with the art of Rosanna Bruno. Here, rendering quite accurately the first ode of the play on a full page, then, on the page facing it, blurring several panels or updating the words in others with interpretations/questions about slavery and sex trafficking, is but one of many ideas that serve to visually portray how modern receptions of the classics tend to work.

American thinkers and artists have drawn upon the classical world in arguing for or sustaining ideas. Edith Hamilton (1964), for instance, clamours for an emulation of ancient Greek thinking in modern American life, with Athens as a model for American democracy, criticizing social institutions of her time – including churches and labour unions – for telling their members how to conduct their affairs. We are headed 'toward a standardization of the mind . . . That was not the Greek way' (Hamilton 1964: 35–6, in Hallett 2016: 227). Such contemplations on civics influenced many US politicians: Robert Kennedy was an avid reader of *The Greek Way* (1930), considering carefully how Hamilton's views could find application under his brother's presidency and later quoting from her translation of Aeschylus' *Agamemnon* in a campaign speech upon learning of Martin Luther King Jr's assassination – as Wilson reminds us in the course of a review of *An Oresteia*, the 2009 volume collecting versions by Carson. Wilson muses that 'While it is hard to imagine then-President Obama citing this particular book in his own speeches', the movement of Carson's trilogy, 'away from the clear ideology of Aeschylus' *Oresteia* toward the much more complex, ambiguous world of Euripides' *Orestes*, seems pertinent to the current political climate. The characters are saved only by divine intervention, and Euripides mocks the notion that law or politics, or any pre-existing system, could prevent catastrophe' (Wilson 2009). The political class may not be so disposed to recognizing the subtleties, as Wilson does here – nor is that the case with poet-translators, on occasion: in a discussion of Tony Harrison's *U.S. Martial* (1981), Blakesley enumerates ways in which, from the very title of this reworking of Martial's epigrams, the British poet systematically redirects translation to cultural and political critique: eliminating, for instance, in one case a proper name and then 'substituting it with the generic "Redneck", an ignorant Southern conservative. This fits in with Harrison's own left-wing politics – and this was, after all, translated during the heyday of Reagan' (Blakesley 2018: 55). Harrison's case is also suggestive of a drawing on the classical world for analogies that extends beyond Robert Kennedy and which involves speeches made by Obama or is encapsulated in how Joe Biden often requotes from the Chorus of Seamus Heaney's version of *Philoctetes* (see Heaney 1991: 135).[9]

---

[9] For just one video of Biden quoting from that passage, see 'Make Hope & History Rhyme: Joe Biden Reads Seamus Heaney', YouTube video, www.youtube.com/watch?v=vc3gyAFCLuA. More extensive quotation from *The Cure at Troy* can be found in one of the ads for his 2020

Similar recognitions occur in posts for the Society for Classical Studies blog, where actual classical translation is seen to be affected just as much: reporting on a panel she co-organized and which was sponsored by the Committee on the Translation of Classical Authors, Diane Rayor shares how most panelists spoke on the ways that contemporary events shape a translation and its reception. In her own case,

> I was revising my translation of *Hecuba* in a production at the University of Colorado, Boulder, this fall during the Kavanaugh hearings, *which shaped the language of Hecuba's response to Odysseus* that 'Those in power should not abuse that power,' as well as Hecuba's argument to Agamemnon against Polymestor's lies ('if someone does evil, his words should be flawed / and not make a persuasive case for injustice'). *My director specifically asked that I see where I could shade the language to resonate with current events.* (Rayor 2019; my emphases)

Such alignments exist and are encouraged: under 'arrangements', one intends a broader, albeit brief, look at certain publication settings, versioning modes, key recontextualizations, and performances in the US context. Theatre is a dominant area in such discourse – and also where, Peter Meineck (2016: 416) points out, a certain bifurcation appears to take place: 'most modern American productions of Greek drama tend to be received as either versions of theatrical rhetoric ("those Greeks were just like us") or radical deconstructions that take an arch, ironic view of the material being presented'. *Dionysus in '69*, the experimental 1968 production of Euripides' *Bacchae* in New York for Richard Schechner's The Performance Group (improvising on the 1959 translation by William Arrowsmith) is emblematic. Under the new title, an obvious reference to both the year of a US presidential election and the sexual position, Schechner's recasting of Euripides sought to activate forces of solidarity, through varied convergences with American art and experience, and the overall metatheatrical inclinations of the project. These included self-referential dialogues developed by the actors employing traditional American children's songs as part of the director's effort to engage the audience and ultimately add its members to the ancient chorus. At the end of the play, 'the limits of the theater space itself were obliterated by an actor-led procession that took the audience dancing out into the streets of SoHo' (Meineck, 2016: 413, drawing on Meineck 2014: 352–83). The chorus as a focus for creativity is singled out in Meineck's survey of classical theatre trends in North America, based on an understanding that 'the representation of a collective body articulating and even

---

presidential campaign: 'The Cure at Troy by Seamus Heaney: Joe Biden for President 2020', YouTube video, www.youtube.com/watch?v=KkCvwvcT1zE.

performing taboo subjects can be viewed as a societal threat to a culture whose narrative art focuses on the trials of the individual, not the group' (Meineck 2016: 416). Yet it is perhaps not tragedy but comedy that should be the subject of adaptations, argues Leezenberg (2007: 269): not only because assimilations that depict George W. Bush as a Creon or Pentheus confer on contemporary rulers 'an aura of aesthetic and moral grandeur that they do not necessarily possess or deserve' but, most importantly perhaps, because with some exceptions (Leezenberg names the *Eumenides* and the *Persians*),

> the extant tragedies are remarkably reluctant to discuss people and events of their own time. It is rather in Aristophanic comedy that we find allusions to contemporary events and politicians, at times with an astonishing frankness. Try and imagine the Bush administration and the collective Pentagon chiefs of staff being present at a theatre performance where their war efforts are being savagely ridiculed in front of the electorate; but this is precisely what Aristophanes did in the midst of the Peloponnesian War. (p. 269)

The political dimension in a US context should be regarded in a wide sense, with further adjectives and emphases relating to particular groups and populations. In the academic environment especially, aspects of race have been debated more prevalently than elsewhere, a case in point being the foregrounding by black classicists such as Dan-el Padilla Peralta of diversity and inclusion concerns in American Classics: besides the limited involvement of scholars of colour, the field has been critiqued for racial thinking and cultural and gender exclusivity in how antiquity is examined. (A much publicized 'merit or race' incident in a panel on 'The Future of Classics', at a joint meeting of the Society for Classical Studies with the Archaeological Institute of America held in San Diego in 2019, threw some of these anxieties into sharp relief.[10])

Concerns regarding gender also increasingly inhabit classical retellings and retranslations. Laura (Riding) Jackson's novelistic account of events in the *Iliad* from Helen's point of view, *A Trojan Ending* (1937), is in a sense a modernist precursor to recent reanimations of female classical characters through the conventions of contemporary fiction from the likes of Madeline Miller. Classical translation is far from unaffected: Wilson (2019) justifies an *Odyssey* where the fact of her being the first woman to have translated it into English 'is not merely an interesting piece of trivia; it is essential to my project' (p. 279) and identifies herself among the feminist classicists communicating with a wider world in which '[t]he dead white men, including Homer, are no

---

[10] For a round-up of reports from that meeting, including accounts of and perspectives on the incident that took place, see: https://classicalstudies.org/scs-blog/ionic007/blog-roundup-reports-reactions-and-reflections-after-scs-annual-meeting.

longer the exclusive property of living white men' (p. 297). What interests us here is the decision *not* to pursue some form of creative classical translation:

> It would be possible for a feminist translator simply not to translate andro-centric texts like the Odyssey. One might, instead, choose to translate the works of neglected non-anglophone, non-white women writers – although there are not many of these surviving in ancient Greek. Or one might choose to produce not a translation, but a creative response to Homer – like Alice Oswald's *Memorial*, or Margaret Atwood's *Penelopiad*. *But if no feminists translate classical texts, then students and general readers will have to rely on translations that inscribe uncritical modern assumptions about sex and gender.* I felt a responsibility to provide Greekless readers with a reliable, *authoritative substitute for the Greek text that would take its complex repre-sentations of social inequality, including gender inequality, more seriously than I felt had been done before.* (p. 282; my emphases)

Classical translation proper is thus argued for as the more essential position from which to illuminate issues of social justice, with sociopolitical comment emerging paratextually and coinciding with the translator's autobiography and circumstances.

When it comes to theatrical space, Powers (2018) summarizes the climate well. She registers that

> a variety of contemporary US theatre artists have been 'resignifying' Greek tragedy and its assumed connection to the colonial past. Their productions have worked to rupture the archive in ways that negate the elitist associations with the genre to address instead cultural, sexual and racial formations in diverse communities from the Boyle Heights cholxs [the Mexican/Chicano community] to disabled veterans. The historical-mythological content com-bination provided by tragedy especially aids this process, for in the ancient world, mythological narratives functioned to create and preserve cultural identity and history, individual and communal. Theatre artists today exploit this function in revising the drama that served as the hallmark of Athenian democracy to develop a new syncretic, mythological mix that reflects the needs, concerns and anxieties of a democracy in the present. (p. 2)

Adamitis and Gamel (2013) examine another key strand, in the form of *engaged theatre*, and the legacy of productions such as Meagher's *Herakles Gone Mad* (2006), Sellars' *The Children of Herakles* (2003), and the rock-musical *Prometheus Bound* (2011), the last two for the American Repertory Theater in Cambridge, Massachusetts. Including tenets of applied theatre but larger in terms of therapeutic focus, these 'engaged classics' have drawn on Shay's work, in particular his *Achilles in Vietnam* (1994) and *Odysseus in America* (2002), where, as Adamitis and Gamel (2013: 284) understand it, he argues that 'theater in Athens arose from the political need to purify, purge and reclarify civic understanding to its returning soldiers, so they could again fulfil the role of citizens of a democracy'. The authors themselves were involved in engaged theatre and performances whose aim was to 'confront, challenge and console' the audience. Their *Ajax* included changes from Sophocles' script along these lines:

> The set and costumes evoked modern-day Afghanistan, with the troops in desert fatigues and Tekmessa in a burka; human prisoners of war were substituted for the animals slaughtered by Ajax; the chorus included female soldiers and Odysseus was played by a woman; and Athena appeared at the end of the play, watching as Ajax's body was carried out while 'Taps' sounded. The lines written by the cast included personal and sometimes critical observations on war. Each of the five performances was prefaced by a scholarly lecture on aspects of the Ajax myth in western culture, and followed by a talkback with the cast and audience. (Adamitis and Gamel 2013: 297)

They are not alone in pursuing this: through Theater of War Productions, founded together with Phyllis Kaufman in 2009, Bryan Doerries has repeatedly connected sites of modern conflict with classical drama – most recently in organizing a July 2022 virtual event with dramatic readings from Aeschylus' *The Suppliants*,[11] poignantly including a chorus of Ukrainian citizens.

Time and again, classical translating becomes an opportunity to indirectly convey the concerns of an American self. As he prepares his translation for the *Dionysiaca* project (see Sections 1 and 4), the poet Mike Lala views the 'Marble sarcophagus with the Triumph of Dionysos and the Seasons', sculptor unknown, in Gallery 162 (containing Greek and Roman objects) of the Metropolitan Museum of Art, New York, the city 'in which I live, in the country to which I was born, and remain, a citizen' ('On Translating Nonnus' 2022: 739). The sculpture presents 'an unruly assembly' – which is also what draws Lala

> to the *Dionysiaca*'s Book 13, to public speech, and to poetry. And it is a fact of language across eras, the transhistorical ur-translative pull of words in excess of literal meaning that makes such a swarm possible. What else could draw these people together, to leave their homes, their families, their parents and lovers and children, their communities, and to form, ill-equipped, the regiments of fighters that would travel, mostly by foot, nearly four-thousand miles to invade a country that by any account but Zeus and Iris' doubtful assertion that its people, in plainly racist terms, were unjust, had little to take from, or offer to, them? Nothing but language, that ancient technology our culture today has largely left in service to the image as it and we regress into a new dark age. ('On Translating Nonnus' 2022: 740)

---

[11] For more information about the project, see the Theater of War website: https://theaterofwar.com/projects/the-suppliants-project.

An empathetic conjoining of experiences across millennia is quickened by the classics; such paratextual recordings of the reading and translating mind continue with a contemplation of human society that both evolves and remains the same; yet these American Homers, or an Ajax retold for war veterans, and reconsiderations of gender through Helen or Hecuba, indicate a clear line to (geo)political or activist concerns.

The Shade of Virgil

Ziolkowski (1993) reminds us of another significant constancy, that of Virgil's *Georgics, Aeneid*, and the *Eclogues* within American letters and cultural life. The latter two especially help us identify key fixations with the epic form: Ziolkowski cites Leo Marx's argument that the encounter of the idyllic with reality that underpins the first eclogue speaks for a governing theme in American literature, while Wiltshire is among several scholars that register how Aeneas, explorer and colonizer, serves as an analogue from the seventeenth century onwards, as the nation expands to the west. Virgilian patterns can therefore be witnessed in a wide range of literary texts, some of them listed by Ziolkowski: from Edmund Don Griffiths' 104-line poem in Latin-inflected epic hexameters, 'Columbus' (1818), to the agrarian values imposed on the Nebraska landscape by the protagonist in Cather's *My Ántonia* a century later in 1918, with its clear debts to the *Georgics*; and we may reach even today's songwriting (for a discussion of lines from Virgil embedded in Bob Dylan's lyrics, see Thomas 2012: 134–59).

Ziolkowski discusses Virgilian influences on the agrarians in poetry as well, notably exemplified through Allen Tate's poems 'Aeneas at New York' (1932) and 'Aeneas at Washington' (1936), the first especially serving as a response to the purist manifesto of Archibald MacLeish and including lines that argue that, since Sophocles, poets have supported political and social causes. Another example would be 'The Mountain' included in Robert Frost's collection *North of Boston* (1914) and analysed as a 'political pastoral' by Ziolkowski, who defends Frost's inclination to make 'his first major political statement in this explicitly Virgilian form. The decision reflects his appreciation that Virgil's *Eclogues*, as the first poems in Latin to deal with contemporary political events, supplied a basic paradigm for much subsequent political poetry' (Ziolkowski 1993: 162). A little more than a century later, in *Poems for Camilla* (2018) by Rachel Hadas, brief excerpts from the *Aeneid*, mostly from Books 6 and 11 and in the original Latin, precede nearly all poems. As I have argued (Nikolaou 2020: 310), '[c]onstants of human behavior can thus be tested or illuminated through quoted words and phrases in Virgil. "Ignorance" is preceded by a quartet of occurrences of *ignarus* across the *Aeneid*, before Hadas unfolds a poignant meditation on its value and existences within moral character.' Virgil's ghostly original frames and amplifies a perspective on American public life, including Donald Trump, in power at the time of publication, his conduct appraised in the last five lives of 'Painted Full of Tongues': 'Crouching in his tower, he pouts and glowers, / angry and happy, happy to be angry, / and keeps on putting forth a froth of words / true and false mixed – but falsehood trumps the truth. / Virgil's *Fama* is female. Not this time' (Hadas 2018: 44). Interviewed about her work, Hadas admits that she used Ruden's 2008 translation of the *Aeneid* as a point of departure and, crucially, 'if I found something in Ruden that I liked, I went straight to the Latin. Sometimes these textual journeys took me to places I hadn't planned to go. For example, I'd find myself transported to Riverside Park, immersed in memories of my father, and from there the text would carry me to Troy and Rome' (Nikolaou 2022a). Here, too, we notice how close 'translation proper' lies to, and often assists in a later, imaginative resituating of analogues of the classical source inside our experience today.

A commemorative function is frequently pursued through Virgil too: especially hard to miss as one enters the 9/11 Memorial Museum in New York, where part of a larger installation titled 'Trying to Remember the Color of the Sky on That September Morning' (2014) by the artist Spencer Finch (Figure 1) announces a key phrase from the *Aeneid* Book 9, the letters forged from pieces of recovered World Trade Center steel and surrounded by watercolour tiles:

Figure 1 Spencer Finch: 'Trying to Remember the Color of the Sky on That September Morning' (2014)

If the quote suggests 'the transformative potential of remembrance' per the description on the museum's website,[12] a sort of camera negative of this strategy is exemplified on the cover of Lombardo's 2005 translation (Figure 2), through an image detail from the Vietnam Memorial in Washington, DC, effectively linking the war dead of then and now: Virgil's meanings, via Lombardo and his publisher, rededicated for an American imperium and reinforced in visual peritext.

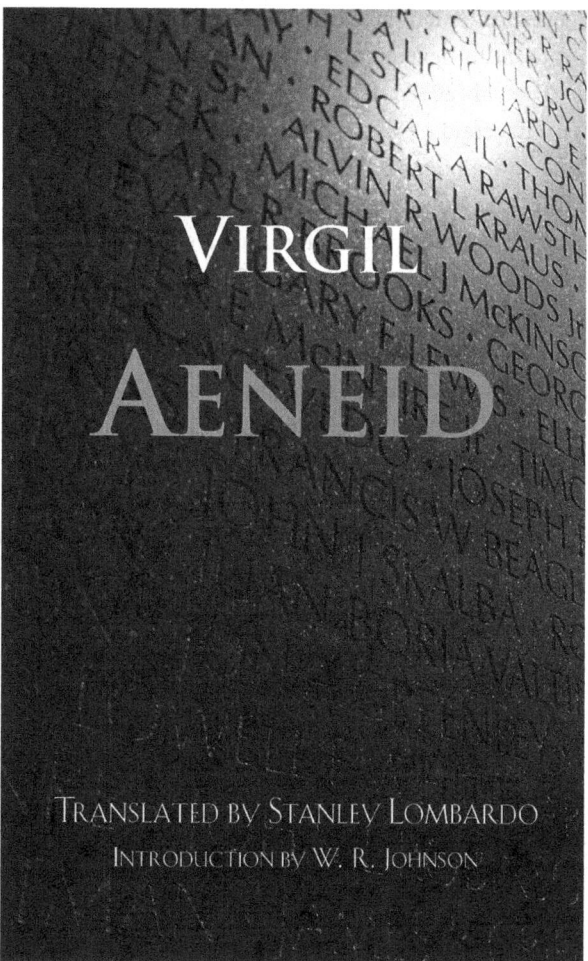

Figure 2 Cover of Virgil, *Aeneid* (2005; Hackett Publishing)

---

[12] 'A Look at the Museum's Memorial Hall', a blog post on the 9/11 Memorial and Museum website gives more details on the artwork: www.911memorial.org/connect/blog/look-museums-memorial-hall.

What is more, when he reviews Oswald's *Memorial*, Green (2012) hypothesizes that the monument influences the British poet who

> clearly haunted by the black granite stretches of the Vietnam Memorial Wall in Washington, with its endless list of names, has conceived the idea of giving the countless casualties mentioned in *The Iliad* a similar list of their own, projected on a kind of virtual memorial wall, thus formalizing their ancient demise through a modern image still raw with suffering.

With Virgil, we may also be reminded how the very reception of actual translations may be laden with requirements for geo- or sociopolitical comment and point to developments in American classical scholarship, an argument that Braund (2018: 107–24) pursues in an essay on Mandelbaum's (Virgil 1971), Fitzgerald's (Virgil 1981), and Fagles' (Virgil 2006), renderings of the *Aeneid* – alongside those by Lombardo and Ruden. The Vietnam conflict occupies the minds of translators, as they exist in dialogue with iterations of the *Aeneid* that came before, and a stance on the war is implied with each subsequent publication. Against the background of the civil rights movement from the mid-1950s onwards, later student activism across American campuses, and the Woodstock Festival, there is a connection between the '1960s questioning of all institutions, political, religious, and intellectual, and in particular with attitudes towards America's own imperialism' and a reaction to earlier readings of the *Aeneid*; the essential message now emerging involved the 'dark side of political success and the cost of imperialism, a cost felt by the victor as well as victim' (Putnam cited in Braund 2018: 108). The discontent, however, that Mandelbaum felt while translating the *Aeneid* and registered in his introduction appears to dissipate a decade later in Fitzgerald's more elevated and formal translation, concentrating on Aeneas' achievement. Braund ventures that this lack of protest may stem from Fitzgerald's experience in active service in the US Navy during the Second World War: he reads the entire poem when stationed on an island in the Pacific in 1945 before participating in the attack on Honshu; what kept him reading, according to his postscript (Fitzgerald 1981: 414) were 'Virgil's descriptions of desperate battle, funeral pyres, failed hopes of truce or peace' – therefore his attitude towards the *Aeneid* was arguably 'shaped many years before he came to translate it, years before Vietnam and the protests' (Fitzgerald 1981, cited in Braund 2018: 113). More than two decades later, the translations by Lombardo and Fagles were not as passionately expected to produce comment on the war, even as certain cues and echoes of that pre-established association – now part of Virgil's reception – remain (the Lombardo cover, no less).

Linkages of the *Aeneid* with the nation's progress make their presence felt in recent translations and their reviews, nevertheless. Commenting on her 2020 translation, Shadi Bartsch acknowledges prior readings, from nineteenth-century Americans seeing Aeneas' westward journey and conquests as resonant with manifest destiny, all the way to the dramatization of the costs of empire in the wake of Vietnam. In 2020, however, she understands the *Aeneid* as a 'sort of propaganda that lets you see it as such, that points to itself and says, you can accept me, maybe I'll be useful for you in making the nation cohere better by giving it a foundation story. But every foundation story also has a cost' (Demanski 2021: 31). In the twenty-first century, Bartsch argues, we are better positioned to recognize what it entails: 'Weeding out things that don't fit in the foundation story, whether it's women's voices, or indigenous voices, or the voices of the people who resist it. Other voices have to be silenced for this voice to exist' (Demanski 2021: 31). Bartsch's introduction further hones a contemporary geopolitical resonance:

> In an age of refugees seeking to escape their war-torn homelands, an age of rising nationalism across the globe; an age in which many in Europe and the United States are suspicious of 'the East' and its religious differences – in our age, that is – the *Aeneid* has more to say to us than ever, especially about the costs (and to be fair, benefits) of national ideologies and the way that myths of origins and heroes are created. (Bartsch 2020: xv)

Versions, Subversions, Fusions, and Redirections

Few instances reflect the intensities of the modernists' conversation with the classics more consequentially than Pound's *The Pisan Cantos* (1948), where a confluence of classical references and transliterated fragments assists the telling of his circumstances in Italy in the aftermath of the Second World War: imprisoned in a Disciplinary Training Center (DTC) north of Pisa by the victorious American forces, the fascist apologist takes stock. Ziolkowski cites Donald Davie's argument that, given the absence of Virgil in *The Cantos* overall, it is especially striking when Pound borrows from Gavin Douglas' 1513 translation of the *Aeneid* 'to make the analogy between Aeneas's departure from Troy and Pound's own flight from Rome at the end of World War II' (Ziolkowski 1993: 191). Another poignant classical allusion is to Hermes, providing the moly that allows Odysseus and his crew to ward off, with memories of their native land, the 'dangerous drugs' (*pharmaka*) that Circe has fed them. Richard Sieburth, the editor of the 2003 edition, points out that the table 'at which Pound the *pharmakos* (or scapegoat) rehearses his remembrances at the DTC is another such gift of trickster god Hermes', who is

'traditionally emblematized by his enchanter's wand – the same caduceus that
adorns the crate of medical or pharmaceutical supplies on which the poet now
writes:

> (O Mercury god of thieves, your caduceus
> is now used by the american army
> as witness this packing case)'
>   (77.220–23; in Pound 2003: xxiii)

Sieburth further reminds us that Odysseus' descent into the underworld, the
'Nekuia' suggested by Pound's notebooks as a key behind Canto 74, was also
the start of the entire project, some thirty years earlier. This episode represented
'the most archaic sediment of Homer's poem, and [Pound's] decision to devote
Canto 1 to a translation of the *katabasis* of Book 11 of the *Odyssey* made it
evident that his modernist epic would similarly have to voyage back into
origins, sacrificing blood to give voice to the shades of the heroic past'
(Pound 2003: xxviii).

Settings of poetry are more accommodating to formal experimentation and
generic hybridity: a preoccupation with the epic tradition often fusing with that
anxious pursuit of the 'great American novel' progresses with poetry into self-
questioning, parodic, and subversive approaches. In the American context,
'post-epic verse-novels provide a self-reflexive space that is aware of their
contentious engagement with post-modernism and post-colonialism, and are
paradoxical and self-reflexive, as they highlight their own ambivalences and
contradictions in order to critique the purported objectivity of epic history and
mythology' (Burkitt 2007: 159). They challenge the epic and its 'spectacle
projection of ideological coherence and routine masking of difference, by being
interactive, fragmentary and elliptical' (p. 161), an approach exemplified in
Omeros (1990) by Walcott and other postcolonial verse-novels that succeeded
it. The tendency is later evident in Carson's *Autobiography of Red* (1998) and its
sequel, *Red/Doc* (2013), where we witness metatextual reconfigurations of
classical material, interwoven modes of expression and commentary, and arguably a twin impulse of salvage and re-creation. Yet intentions and priorities may
vary greatly: Cyrus Console's *The Odicy* (2011) is an experimental sequence on
ecological crisis whose author has admitted drawing on the epic mode for its
survivability, and its goal as an adaptation is not, according to Eccleston (2019:
23; my emphasis), 'to tell the Odyssean narrative, but to *enact a consideration
of Odyssean questions* regarding language, signification, and recognition given
current political economies of language in the USA'.

Postdramatic stagings also helped express traumatic experience in modern
US history, inadvertently even, as in The Wooster Group's *To You, The Birdie!*

(2001): this was based on Racine's *Phèdre*, itself drawing upon *both* Euripides' and Seneca's treatment of the myth. *To You, The Birdie!* followed for the most part the narrative established by the two ancient tragedians through a reduced English adaptation by Paul Schmidt that exists in dialogue with an array of multimedia elements further externalizing the palimpsest constitution of the play-text. This facilitates critical distance, argues Cole (2020); in a typical scene involving Hippolytus and Theramenes, the audience is made aware of two characters 'reflected and refracted through a Perspex wall, a television monitor, and a microphone, and mediated via Euripides, Seneca, Racine, the performers, and additional unseen forces' (p. 155). What is more, performances were scheduled to begin a fortnight after the 9/11 attacks – and in the very same venue used by Schechner decades earlier. Given how *Dionysus in '69* also opened the day after Robert Kennedy's assassination, Cole (2020: 148) makes the point that 'socio-political events colour the theatre and provide prisms through which audiences read action regardless of authorial intent'. Her quote from a 2010 review essay by Jakovljevic amply illustrates this:

> Less than a mile from the site of the World Trade Center, the streets of lower SoHo were still covered with a film of fine white ash. The air smelled of burning fuel and plastic, in which many claimed to detect the odor of scorched – or as Genet would have it, 'cooked' – human flesh. The only moment of profound and immediate resonance between the incomplete theatre piece and the fractured world in which it was placed so directly and so improbably was the moment when Theseus, played by Willem Dafoe, was seen onstage, lying down on a stretcher made of bright orange fabric, identical to the ones that crews of paramedics were hopelessly carrying around the smoldering ruins, still looking for bodies that were not completely pulverized. (Jakovljevic 2010: 88, in Cole 2020: 148)

The collective trauma of 9/11 led to a flurry of artistic responses, from sculpture and public art to photography and literature. Such art often embeds within it questions of *how* to respond, and translations and adaptations provide a possible answer, along with the space for recognitions. One instance is 'Horace and the Thunder', a translation of *Odes* 1.34 by Seamus Heaney, published in the immediate aftermath of the terrorist attacks in *The Irish Times* (17 November) (Heaney 2001a). Such recourse to the cultural authority of classical authors in acts of commemoration does not fall far from the function served by that Virgil quote installed years later close to the entrance of the 9/11 Memorial and Museum. Heaney chooses this ode to ventriloquize a sense of 'poetry's covenant with the irrational ... thunder in the clear, blue sky', as he puts it in an interview, since in the original, Jupiter 'can bring the unknown forward. And this moment of great danger, great grief, great dread, promised a re-tilting of the world in all kinds of ways' (Heaney and O'Driscoll 2003). It resonates with the present that Heaney contemplates, and his version also arrives in a period that finds the poet deeply involved with classical material, as several items included in *Electric Light* (Heaney 2001b) attest to. Naming author and theme in the title makes us aware of intertext and translational variation to follow; and Heaney's move to remind us of this ode after 9/11 is amplified by ways in which 'Horace and the Thunder' deviates from the original: of the four stanzas published, the last one ('Ground gives. The heavens' weight / Lifts up off Atlas like a kettle lid, / Capstones shift, nothing resettles right. / Telluric ash and fire-spores boil away', 13–16) belongs to Heaney, yet written in the key of Horace and more directly summoning 9/11 imagery. This response-through-translation itself evolves and is re-echoed. The impactful phrase 'Anything Can happen: after Horace *Odes* 1.34' is foregrounded and mention of the Roman poet occurs later – and presaged by 'after' – when the work is republished by Amnesty International as *Anything Can Happen: A Poem and Essay by Seamus Heaney with Translations in Support of Art for Amnesty* (Heaney 2004a) along with twenty-three translations into languages from Afrikaans to Hindi and Greek; such an exponentiation of an ancient poem that Heaney has already modified and recontextualized in English stages a likeness of shocked reaction shared across nations and cultures. The resulting multiples of 1.34 collectively iterate Heaney's initial thematic realization and confirm it through a palimpsest of voices. Translation here is individual and collective *action* in the service of cultural memory, aiming to impress a common response on readers' minds.

A few years later, it is theatrical space that instils awareness of diachronic wartime dilemmas, foremost in Heaney himself, when the Abbey Theatre commissions a new version of *Antigone*: 'President Bush and his secretary of defence were forcing not only their own electorate but the nations of the world into an either/or situation with regard to the tyrant of Baghdad. If you were not for state security to the point that you were ready to bomb Iraq, you could be represented as being in favour of terrorism' (Heaney 2009: 133). While these circumstances, Heaney argues, would have made it easy to proceed with a treatment 'where Creon would have been a cipher for President Bush and the relationship between audience and action would have been knowing and predicated on the assumption of political agreement' (p. 134), to go in this direction 'would have been reductive and demeaning, both of Sophocles' art and of the huge responsibility the White House must bear for national security' (p. 134). Moreover, the poet's own statements (beyond Heaney 2009, see also Heaney 2005) alert reviewers of what was retitled *The Burial at Thebes* (Heaney 2004b), as well as Heaney scholars, to the connective tissue between geopolitical reality and Heaney translating (see esp. Wilmer 2007: 228–42 and Parker 2019: 98–120).

It is far from the only *Antigone* to mirror the geopolitical context after 9/11 or be performed outside the United States. *Antigone: Insurgency*, subtitled *Sophocles Revisited*, was directed by Adam Seelig in Toronto in 2007 as a response to widespread security measures after 9/11. Seelig presents us with a radical reworking that integrates the discourse of the recent past: as one discussion of the performance points out, the script 'treated Sophocles' text as a score into which modern material was interpolated. For example, Creon's first speech drew on both that of George Bush at ground zero on 14 September, and another by Canada's former Prime Minister Pierre Trudeau' (Chang 2011: 267).

Ancient texts will fuse with the experiences and art forms of American communities across a disparate geography: in one of many examples, Gregory Jusdanis encounters a hip-hop group in the streets of Ohio's capital, Columbus: Nes and the Thousand mingled hip-hop, classical music, and Mediterranean sounds in an improvisation of words and music that to Jusdanis' ears 'was Homeric, a street performance without previous planning. It had its roots in a time when art was part of life, not something detached and termed "art"' (Jusdanis 2017). He proceeds to ask Nes Wordz (Sheron Colbert) to compose an episode of the *Odyssey* for his class at university 'to demonstrate how Homer might have functioned in his own society' (Jusdanis 2017). Nes 'seemed taken by the possibility of not simply reciting Homer in hip-hop rhythms – that would have been easy – but of reimaging the Greek bard, of setting him in the "hood," in Columbus, of translating his language in Nes's own idiom' (Jusdanis 2017). In a partial draft from *The Black Odyssey* that resulted from this process,[13] these intentions become clear, as we are told about a combative Big O (Odysseus) and One-eyed P (Polyphemus): 'I'm a man, tryna reap the spoils of the land, with a big torch placed in my hand' or asserting, 'From a fight I never ran, I fought many battles and I didn't lose a hand, hopped out the Trojan horse and guns went blam, flawless victory, I'll make you a memory, I'm a king so I know they envy me?' We may concur with Jusdanis that Odysseus here 'is made into an arrogant "gangsta," someone selfishly moving through the neighborhood for his own benefit, subjecting everyone around him to his own experience and domination' (Jusdanis 2017). Talking to the students, the hip-hop artist communicates his hope to 'rewrite the entire *Odyssey* and then take it to schools to bring the classics to the street, to unify the high and low, the abstract and the concrete, the black and white' (Jusdanis 2017).

---

[13] The text of this partial draft by Nes Wordz can be found in Jusdanis (2017).

Theatrical space is not immune from similar instillations of music genres, one example being the reworking of Aeschylus' *Seven Against Thebes* by the hip-hop artist Will Power in 2007. Production was spurred because Power felt it could serve as a comment on the effect of absent fathers on the African American community (see Meineck 2016: esp. 417–20), and in this thematic context the ancient chorus could also be reconceived as a reflection of the verbal dexterity and rhyming of hip-hop: in performance, the chorus was even led by a DJ spinning turntables. More crucially, Power's adaptation combined with 'filliping', as he himself described his creative method – *also* drawn from hip-hop. The creator of *The Seven* proceeded to blend Vellacott's translation of Aeschylus from 1954 with references from popular culture, music, art, and literature – again, actual translation as springboard: metabolized and versioned through the use of other intertexts, art forms, and genres. Meineck (2016: 418) further draws attention to the fact that '[t]he heightened language of Vellacott combined with the slang and vernacular of Hip-Hop created a dynamic tension between old and new that reinforced the notion that the cast was telling an ancient story. This accentuated the status of the story of Oedipus and his family as a living myth – something vital and important that needed to be told.' Further musical genres were layered in and juxtaposed to create meaning: 'in one scene, Power used African-American spiritual songs and early Blues riffs to evoke a sense of history and isolation at the place where the three roads met. At other times, the live band played Funk, Jazz, R&B and Rap music, driving the show with considerable force' (p. 418).

Such co-occurrences of ancient drama and musical theatre are resonant of an attitude to artistic endeavour that is appreciably American. The Jazz pianist Marcus Roberts expresses this aptly, in conversation with the Berlin-based violinist Daniel Hope, for the liner notes of an album that draws from the American songbook. Classical music and jazz intertwine in *America* (2022), where the genres, according to Roberts, are felt to 'represent two different views of creativity and humanity' and ask for certain compromises as they are brought together. The ability, however, 'to learn from each other's classical perspective gives both art forms, in my opinion, even more power and validity' (Hope and Roberts 2022: 12). Earlier in the same conversation, Roberts defines American music as already symbolizing an essential quality 'which is about flexibility, the ability to adapt, and to consciously – and constantly – create and recreate' (p. 7). Music simply parallels that energy, we are told. Several of the approaches to classical translation discussed in this section can also be thought about in this key, perhaps: more sensitive to a nation's progress and place in the world, cognizant of tensions in society, and often existing as applications of cultural theory, these American (re)arrangements occur more prosperously through a collision of art forms and genres – the result often representing the fusion of cultural experiences and moral or ideological stances in dialogue.

4 Paratextual Possessions

The Translation(s) in the Paratext

The philosopher William Godwin tells Charles Lamb that the preface of the then soon to be published *The Adventures of Ulysses* (1808) 'ought I think to tell what Homer was – the Father of poetry, the eldest of historians, the collector & recorder of all that was then known, the parent of continuous narration, of imagery, of dramatic character, of dramatic dialogue, of a whole having beginning, middle & end' (in Webb 2004: 290). Such are the chronological and cultural distances involved that modern readers must be ushered into the frame of a period in classical antiquity, become acquainted with a moral universe unlike their own, the experiences of the original audience or readers, and also know about the intertexts, allusions, and reworkings that see classical authors in dialogue and may serve as points of transition between ancient Greece and Rome. Length is perhaps to be expected: the introduction by Bernard Knox to the Fagles translation of the *Odyssey* totals sixty-eight pages and includes notes on the ancient hero and the place of Gods and women in the age of Homer before further pages are dedicated specifically to the spelling and pronunciation of names and maps of Homeric geography. Another fifty pages follow the translation, featuring copious lists of textual variants, genealogies, and a pronouncing glossary, but these sections begin with a 'Translator's Postscript' (Fagles 2001: 419–26) where Fagles relates his intention to vary his voice in more ways than in his earlier translation of the *Iliad*, 'modulating it to fit the postwar world, the more domestic, more intimate world of the later poem' (p. 420). Still, he seeks middle ground, since 'the more literal approach would seem too little English, and the more literary seems too little Greek. What I have tried to find is a cross between the two, a modern English Homer' (p. 420). An appreciation not only of several modern translators of Homer ('[e]ach has introduced me to a new aspect of the poem, another potential for the present', p. 423) but of a long list of fellow poets, novelists, and classicists follows: from Wallace Stevens to Joyce Carol Oates and to Richard Martin.

Permutations of translator statements and introductions by classicists are not limited to meeting readers' needs for context in 'proper' translations, as is the case with the Fagles *Odyssey* but even when translation and freer regimens coexist. It happens in *After Callimachus: Poems* (2020), whose pages see Stephanie Burt (2020: xxii) 'reflect, interpret, adapt, respond to, and sometimes simply translate the poems, and parts of poems, that the ancient poet

Callimachus wrote'. The hybridity in her approach becomes clearer a few sentences later (the title of her paratext, 'Imitator's Note', is telling):

> [T]he English verses in this book should not be mistaken for consistently accurate scholarly translations. *Such translations already exist.* Some of the English here closely imitates or directly translates Callimachus's Greek. Much of it does not. In adapting Callimachus's surviving complete poems and (even more so) his many fragments, *I have made cuts, expanded on his metaphors, provided new metaphors, fleshed out situations he leaves implicit, imposed other situations whose modern details the original Alexandrian could not have imagined, based English phrases as much on the sounds of the Greek as on its literal sense,* and sometimes aggressively modernized his world. If this book is a work of translation (and I hope it is!), it's also science fiction, or alternative history. (p. xxii; my emphases)

And yet the motive behind such wild combinations appears to be a more appropriate re-encounter of Callimachean sensibility: a 'hyper-conscious' translation. Burt may not intend a 'historically and linguistically precise reconstruction of his poems in their original Alexandrian and Hellenistic contexts' (p. xxii) but her goal remains, 'a new Callimachus', one that exists 'in a world with twenty-first-century technology, though his world is not our own. He and his coevals fly on airplanes, send email and Tweets' (p. xxii).

Beyond providing ample details about Callimachus' own life, work, and reception, it is left to the classicist Mark Payne to fasten Burt's versioning to literary history and to Callimachus' antecedents and inheritors. He notes how modernist poets indeed 'reveled in the imaginative possibilities of the minimal fragment' (Payne 2020: xiv) and proceeds to use an illustrative example of Callimachus' '274', from *Hecale* (in Payne's literal rendition: 'A light fuzz was just getting going on that youth / resembling a golden flower', p. xiv) that turns to a whole 'transhistorical drama of becoming male', totalling twelve lines in the hands of Burt. It is also telling how he connects Burt's abilities as translator to the epigrams present in her earlier poetry (2006 and 2013), but not before emphasizing that the creative result from the *Hecale* fragment still aligns with an objective of Callimachus translated:

> It's an expansion, obviously, but not in the mode of bloviation, and we should pause for a moment to consider what it means to be able to expand so successfully on a poet who valued concision as much as Callimachus did. The fragment has regrown itself from its damaged stock, and become the thing it was always meant to be. We see more in the original than we could have seen without the expansion, but seeing more does not violate the integrity of the original. The translation brings out the truth of the original. It is the bloom of its hidden being. (Payne 2020: xv)

In other cases, translator and classical scholar remain the same person and the dialogue between the two capacities is no less interesting for it: after ensuring that readers are cognizant of Catullus' biography, the relationships with other poets, and key aspects of his language and style, Balmer's introduction to *Catullus: Poems of Love and Hate* (2004) features a series of 'notes to self' – yet ones that readers must hear, too. '[J]ust as Catullus subverted Sappho's essentially female poetics in his cross-gendered versions, so there might have been a temptation here, as a 21st century woman, to subvert Catullus' male Roman sensibilities, overwriting them with an implicit, if playful, challenge to his imagery of domination and submission' (Balmer 2004b: 24). After noting that very few women have been drawn to Catullus, Balmer concludes that his poetry 'was already quite subversive enough. And perhaps, as a woman, I could not take his belligerent posturing too seriously. But then neither, one suspects, did Catullus' (p. 24).

Part of why we come across exhaustive commentary alongside classical translation relates to the fact that any instance of it would, more likely than not, be a retranslation – and thus keenly orienting itself towards the original, its existing translators, and the nature of the translating act itself. Some paratexts will thereafter traverse eons, removed from the translation they served. The contents of volumes like Douglas Robinson's *Western Translation Theory from Herodotus to Nietzsche* (2002), or the first chapters of the Lawrence Venuti-edited *The Translation Studies Reader* (2004) suggest the extent to which such reflection forms the prehistory of translation studies. Different translation approaches resulted from reaction to what had come before: exchanges between (poet-)translators often continuing from the realm of private correspondence to becoming published statements, like Jerome's letter to Pammachius, written in AD 395. Commentary also extends beyond the boundaries of books: we hardly encounter paratexts in Pound's work, as some have noted. Even as he 'found the poetic not only in the art of translation but in the scholarship surrounding it' since 'translating was not only a new way of writing out of the text into new poetry but also a way back in to that original text in order to understand it afresh' (Balmer 2013: 48), Pound's theoretical views mostly arrive in the form of letters or literary essays.

An ambiguous issue with Genette's foundational work on paratexts (appearing in English in 1997), and presciently explored by Batchelor (2018), concerns the ways in which translations themselves are already paratexts – given that, according to Genette, the author of the translated text is the author of the original text (see Batchelor 2018: 21). At the same time, if we go by Genette's (1997: 9) categorization, paratexts can also be 'allographic', that is, 'written by [a] third party and accepted by the author' so these may involve, for example, the prefaces of translations. Notwithstanding that essential obstacle of a Homer-approved preface, Genette adds a context in which '[t]he translator-preface writer may possibly comment on, among other things, his own translation; on this point, and in this sense, his preface then ceases to be allographic' (p. 264). In this sense, authorship of a translation is predicated, or certainly intensifies, through the existence of paratexts – of *self-comment*, that is, on the work of translation. It is not surprising that feminist translation strategies as put forward by Simon (esp. Simon 1996) and von Flotow (esp. von Flotow 1997) include the heavy use of autobiographical commentary and paratextual elements in actively registering the translator's subjectivity and as part of concerted action, along-side interventions in the translation itself, towards drawing attention to gender and related issues.

Those more personal, idiosyncratic anthologies of classical translation might still feature paratexts, in defence of the creativity within: there is, for instance, both an introduction and a postscript when John Frederick Nims publishes *Sappho to Valery: Poems in Translation* (1971). He echoes many other practi-tioners when he offers that 'I am not sure that the enjoyment I had in doing these translations is very different from that of writing one's "own poetry"' (Nims 1971: xvii). Soon after, he recognizes dynamics involved when the translator is himself a poet ('there will always be a clash of personalities, with the personal-ity of the translator tending to take over', p. xxi). Such material serves to accent the re-creative concerns often coexisting with a translating process. Eavan Boland's afterword to the American edition of Oswald's *Memorial* (Boland 2012) reminds us that Boland's own verse – *and* translations – are preoccupied with the matter of war and ancient myth. A key stop arguably in her body of work is *After Every War* (2004), translations of nine German poets chosen to thematically attach to Boland's experience of conflict. Boland's venturing into the Ceres and Persephone myth continues here as well, as Trachsler (2021) finds through Boland's (2011) own essay, 'Translating the Underworld', in which the poem 'Frühling 1946' by Elizabeth Langgässer is described, indeed, as 'a note from the underworld. It is the first signal from Ceres that she has found her child. All the rest can come later' (Boland 2011: 96, quoted in Trachsler 2021: 49). This identification 'between the German poet and the ancient goddess allows the translator in turn to relate to her experience, because Boland herself wrote poems in which she identified with the same figure' (Trachsler 2021: 49). Paratexts like 'Translating the Underworld' enable poet-translators to imply those subtle and intimate bonds of life and (translated) text and enable us to complete a picture of their motives.

Anne Carson is a case in point: her work on *An Oresteia* (2009), comprising three plays of a 'non-foundational' cycle that Carson translated at different points in time, is explained and amplified in her introduction through references to modern art – our relationship with photography, for instance, or how the paintings of Francis Bacon connect to Aeschylus (see Carson 2009: 4). Time and again, a poetic sensibility provides solutions to problems of translation. She poignantly relates how anxious she was about conveying the voice and language of Kassandra, imagining a play where 'someone like Björk would sing wild translingual songs while sailing down a snowy river of ancient Asia Minor' (p. 4). Or Carson adopts the voice of Euripides and imagines his response to his critics at the end of *Grief Lessons: Four Plays* (2006). There, an inventive 'Why I Wrote Two Plays about Phaidra' (Carson 2006) operates as dramatization of how an ancient tragedian can be inhabited by – or possess – the translator (see also Nikolaou 2022b: 122).

We register another kind of communion in the paratexts accompanying Heaney's rendering of Book 6 of the *Aeneid* which present how the poet-translator communes with his readers: Heaney's (2016) three-page 'Translator's Note' begins by stressing that this is not a version or crib but a 'classics homework' (p. vii) and ends in an image of the 'writer of verse' who translates the portion from the *Aeneid* as someone that 'has other things than literal accuracy in his mind and in his ear, metre and lineation, the voice and its pacing, the need for diction that is decorous enough for Virgil but not so antique as to sound out of tune with a more contemporary idiom. All the fleeting, fitful anxieties that afflict the literary translator' (p. ix). Between these two points, the decision to translate is explained in autobiographical terms: Heaney started on a translation after his father died, drawn to the description of Anchises' descent into the Underworld in Book 6 and encounter with his father there. Yet this work, dating from the mid-1980s, languished for many years before Heaney re-embarked on the project, following the birth of a first granddaughter in 2007. Parallel to it exists the 'mythic method' that best describes 'Route 110' (Heaney 2010), an autobiographical sequence Heaney published within *Human Chain* and which 'plotted incidents from my own life against certain well-known episodes in Book VI' (Heaney 2016: viii). The poetically inclined partial translation of the *Aeneid* and the classically inspired poetic sequence, he admits, spring from the same root.

A second paratext follows Heaney's translation, written by his daughter, Catherine, with Matthew Hollis. They remind us that after the poet's death in 2013 what is now published emerged by triangulating two drafts left behind and the proofs from a limited, letterpress edition the poet was working on with a typographer. This 'Note on the Text' (Heaney and Hollis 2016: 51–3) begins by citing the italicized first few sentences of Heaney's own unfinished after-word. As for the translation, Hollis and Catherine Heaney remind us of its provisional nature: that we are given a 'final', rather than 'finished', draft. These paratexts – including Heaney's fragment of an afterword – effectively relay to us how the translation project that began as the poet dealt with the death of his father can now echo Heaney's own passing. In a somewhat similar case, Christopher Reid brings us closer to the desk of a deceased poet in his afterword to the definitive edition of Logue's *War Music*. There is a glimpse of what would have been when Reid describes a projected final volume that 'would have subsumed the whole of *War Music* itself, adding both preceding and subsequent incidents, and inserting at least one detail of the story omitted from previous editions: the fashioning of Achilles' new shield and armour' (Reid 2015: 299). But what remains of the poet-translator's ambition is merely a typed note: 'The new shield's face is covered with designs that show the world as Homer knew it. This passage will be extended. The pictures on the shield will reflect our world' (p. 299).

Nor is it only in book form that the classics may be consulted. 'Like Sheep: On Translating a Literary Plague in a Time of Pandemic' opens the winter 2021 issue of *The Hudson Review* and finds A. E. Stallings rendering into English an extract from Book 3 of Virgil's *Georgics*. This is immediately preceded by commentary that links up the Virgil passages with other key mentions of plagues in Homer, Sophocles, Thucydides, Lucretius, and Hesiod. But it was Covid–19 and 'the pandemic in the air that made me want to revisit this classical plague' (Stallings 2021: 544). And it is the actual process of translation that enables her to confront why the passage is 'still often so moving, so immediate despite its obvious artifice and even its sentimentality' (p. 544). Creative choices follow: Stallings deviates from Virgil's unrhymed dactylic hexameter, producing a translation in rhymed iambic pentameter couplets, because 'rhyme is for me a method of composition, a way of making myself look at larger units of syntax and meaning than the line, of understanding the poem' (p. 546). Even more indicative of the emotions and recontextualizing involved, and of translation-as-response, Stallings concludes her presentation of this partial rendering with a wish for totality – indeed, she has since decided to work on a complete translation – and noticeably moving into language that simultaneously confirms current experience as motivation and is visibly more expressive.

Force in Numbers

In 2002, *Horace, The Odes: New Translations by Contemporary Poets*, finds the editor J. D. McClatchy (2002: 5) assembling the 'leading poets of the day' to bring 'different imaginative energies to bear on a joint project ... Horace, in fact, thought of himself as a translator, and considered his true distinction to have been a "gift for turning Greek verse into Latin," an ability to adapt old ways to new times. It was in that spirit that the poets in this book worked.' The range of approaches is emphasized in the introduction: 'Some poets worked close to the Latin bone, sometimes in the original meter. Others wrote more freely: Horace's stanzas are reshaped, rhymes are added or free verse deployed, the looser rhythms of English verse dominate. *This is as it should be*' (pp. 5–6; my emphasis). Creative classical translation manifests here as a spectrum: together, these dissimilar English iterations of the *Odes* affirm Horace's modernity. And, as happens with the Lombardo and Levitan project, each poetic sensibility is enabled to submit its own technique to the classical poet's preoccupations. 'The variety of tone to be heard in the translations', McClatchy suggests,

> matches the mercurial shifts in mood and response the Latin poems themselves exhibit. The pairings of poem and *translator were deliberate, and made in the hope of creating interesting juxtapositions*. To have an American poet laureate write about political patronage, to have a woman poet write about seduction, an old poet write about the vagaries of age, a Southern poet about the blandishments of the countryside, a gay poet about the strategies of 'degeneracy' . . . these are part of the editorial plot for this new book. (p. 6; my emphasis)

Twenty years later, the diversity of paratextual material, and how essential it may be in defending the licences taken, is evident in *Tales of Dionysus: The* Dionysiaca *of Nonnus of Panopolis* (2022), announced on the cover as a 'group translation'. Calling himself a 'son of Homer', Nonnus wrote a mythological epic comprising forty-eight books in dactylic hexameter, albeit diverse in terms of the action and tone, with a wealth of allusions and intertexts. Translators were confounded by such sprawling work, and Rouse produced the only complete translation, for the Loeb Classical Library, between 1940 and 1942; other attempts, including Douglass Parker's unpublished rendering of Book 1 and the first 162 lines of Book 2 in 1970, were partial and sparse. Lombardo and Levitan – both students of Parker's – admit in their editors' preface that the unfinished translation served as impetus for a complete *Dionysiaca*. This is a poem, however, that keeps shifting shape: 'Out of its formal epic frame spills a tumult of ancient literary types: tragedy, elegy, didactic, panegyric, pastoral idyll, and the novel are all parts of this gigantic enterprise, each genre and its ancient instances coming to the fore one after the other' (Levitan and Lombardo 2022: xiv). Inviting translators from different backgrounds, classical scholars, poets, or both, to provide an English version for each book seemed an apt way 'to render, even if perhaps *to amplify*, the poem's protean nature' (p. xiv; my emphasis). Creativity therefore begins here with how the editors approach this polyphony; the overall design demands translational experiment.

The array of voices and translational experiment is also captured in a nearly thirty-page section towards the end of the tome which contains statements by participants on the many refigurations that come about as translation turns into poetry. 'On Translating Nonnus' stands as a paratextual bestiary of creativity: for Book 2, Levitan takes it upon himself to complete Parker's work, but his continuation of translation is simultaneously a debt repaid and a course adjusted: whereas Parker's Nonnus 'bursts onto the scene in explosions of language, style, genre, literary history, and even typeface' ('On Translating Nonnus' 2022: 743), Levitan responds by 'lowering the temperature', not least in his capacity as editor ('My thought was to lay down a rhetorical floor far enough below Parker's de facto ceiling to open the most capacious space for the full cavalcade of translations to come', p. 743). And, given the ways in which the original glances at *Iliad* 10, Levitan argues that he is justified in borrowing some lexical elements from a previous English translation. He is not alone: Gordon Braden incorporates allusions in his rendering of Book 24, with the presence of Leonard Cohen, Frank Sinatra, or Walter Cronkite intended *to supplement and echo* Nonnus' 'carpet of literary allusions with quotations from my own more recent cultural memory' (p. 730). Braden makes subtractions and additions across his translation: 'The former are signaled in the text, and the reason for them should be obvious. The signals themselves constitute additions, making explicit the kind of literary self-reference everywhere operating in the Greek' (p. 730). For his part, Turner's response to the 'mad, intertextual work' that Nonnus produces must be a 'forceful decentering' of the existing English translation by Rouse,

> drowning it out with other voices. At the center of the book I was translating lay Nonnus' spin on the Actaeon story, so I started listening to Charpentier (Op. H481) and Purcell (Z. 626), picking at snippets of translations of Callimachus and Euripides, and – in particular – wandering the Theban sections of Arthur Golding's *Metamorphoses*, looking for tips from the text that Ezra Pound saw as 'the most beautiful book in the English language'. (p. 751)

Creating this distance from Rouse also means moving towards the Greek, which Turner tries to do by recording his own recitation of the original, writing a verbatim gloss and then sitting to listen 'to my tongue-tied Greek while leafing through eighteen pages of mangled English' (p. 751). Nor is intertextuality restricted to readings or loans: other *Dionysiaca* translators do not know ancient Greek, and their versions are developed by metabolizing earlier renderings. To simultaneously consult, and abstract from, the Rouse translation is to see creative choices catalyse, as the retranslation moves away from the bedrock of the English in the 1940–2 edition. Anderson now felt justified in stating that

'As I am a poet and not a scholar of ancient Greek, I wanted to convey a slice of this startling epic as felt by a modern reader. Such an interpretation requires looking through a long telescope of history, to see the tumultuous present layered by a vivid past' (pp. 726–7). Anderson feels it was important 'to reflect a witness to these horrors, and so I included a narrator's voice, the "I" behind the subtitle. Taking liberty, I inserted a few lines not found in the original, *ones I thought were implied by the verse*' (p. 727; my emphasis). Considering that Nonnus' self-consciousness about literary tradition 'by its very nature brings with it an often inscrutable sense of detachment from that tradition', Braden decides to compose his own translation in *ottava rima*, notably 'a prosodic form associated in European poetry since the Renaissance with a similar sense of epic operating at a certain distance from itself' (p. 729).

Denise Low attacks the material from multiple points. Not only does she parse her rendition of Book 28 into subtitled sections; she also compresses 'the original content of the epic, subtracting from the original Greek' (p. 744) – an attitude seen in much other creative translating, Logue's *War Music* for one. Low is conscious of the metaphorics of the process she is engaged in. Book 28 presents readers with a battle between Greek and Indian armies, and so the translator's page 'is another kind of battlefield, with losses suggested by open spaces – omissions of lines. In finding the lyric nugget within a scene, I cut much away, in a series of erasures' (p. 744). As observed in previous sections of this Element, a metatextual iconicity attends creative classical translating, especially in Low's second contributed translation, of Book 38, where this sense finds the thematic ground in which to accelerate and encounters the translator's own life: 'At the climax of Phaëthon's prideful journey', writes Low,

> he overturns the order of the sky. Here, I break with the orderly hexameter lines to approximate chaos on the page, using jumbled typology and keyboard characters. At first, I tried using astrological glyphs, but these did not repro- duce consistently in print media, so I turned to carets, parentheses, and tildes. Ovid describes Chaos as the confusion of elements, and I include words and letters. My alphabetic representation of words is interrupted by special characters used out of context. I had hoped to make spirals of individual lines on the page, but chose instead a more stable linear format, but erratic, which still replicates the idea of chaos in broken lines. Ptolemy's astrology, which antecedes the contemporary practice, informs this section; I have practiced astrology over fifty years. (p. 745)

Here is a glimpse of what this thinking results in:

Eos the Dawn walks deep space   **O**

The blue-hot star Sirius leaps at the Big Bear, *Ursa Major*, scorching its fur.   ++   /\\   ++

The two fishes of Pisces   < / >
   one headed North
   the other South

break apart.
</   />

(Levitan and Lombardo 2022: 570–1)

In the earlier translation of Book 28, and similar to Turner listening to Prokofiev, the creative translator reaches for a soundscape. Here, Low searches for diachronies of dance and finds a video of cadets of the Hellenic Army Academy performing the Pyrrhic war dance in the present:[14] the music 'played in the background as I worked on the translation. The description of the military parade to battle, then, gained more dimensions as I worked on my own recomposition process, even if that music does not sound overtly' ('On Translating Nonnus' 2022: 745). That process is described as a 'patchwork' essentially developed from 'Rouse's translation; my rudimentary Greek (I had one inglorious semester); consultation with handbooks of mythology; and a lifetime's study of verse' (p. 746). Low's meditation on dance and/as dialogue is also consonant with her decision to enlist a further voice inside her own translation: Eileen R. Tabios is asked to produce brief italicized responses which are then *embedded* in Low's version, as in the following section from Book 28:

Heroes Fall
One unbelievable sight was a corpse
still standing in place, bristling with arrows,
a flesh statue still poised to throw a lance.

An Athenian lost both arms and said,
"What I want is a third hand to keep fighting."
He rushed into enemy swords and fell.

Horsemen died according to will of the Fates—some
dragged, some thrown, some speared.
Every fighter gambled his life. Many lost.

    Manhood when defined
    as dying into a stance
    "poised to throw a lance"
    begets poetry, but who
    needs such impotent Beauty?

(Levitan and Lombardo 2022: 441)

---

[14] The video that Low finds inspiring as to her own process can be found on YouTube: 'Greek War Dance, Bloody & Violent (Pyrrhic Dance)', www.youtube.com/watch?v=cYelSpTWVUw.

Their added layer of counterpoint and collaboration reflects a way in which poetry, 'from Homer to the present, is a shared genre, incomplete without a reader and at least one responder if a chorus is not available' ('On Translating Nonnus' 2022: 746). Low closes her comment on what has become a rethinking and resituating of translation with a reminder of how translational licence may also be encouraged by considerations of scholarship: '"The study of ancient epic in its earliest form has revealed the connection between performance and the creation of verse: composition and performance in oral poetry are aspects of the same process, in that each performance is an act of recomposition" (in Gregory Nagy's phrase). This translation, too, both reprises and recomposes' (p. 746).

Classical Paratexts As Performance

Chapman defends the use of 'periphrases' by those that came before him in the poem that precedes his translated *Iliad*. In verse, he argues that they all lacked the art, 'With poesy to open poesy – / Which in my poem of the mysteries / Revealed in Homer I will clearly prove . . .' (Chapman 2005: 26). Several poet-translators today continue in this vein, the critical accompaniment to a translation transforming from necessary tool to an auxiliary creative section. Accounting for the process turns into a field of artistic justification and re-enactment, a field in which creativity is enabled and resumes.

The other side of this coin involves the effects that paratexts produce in projects of fiction or poetry that aim to re-narrate literary moments from the classical world. The afterword in Ursula K. Le Guin's *Lavinia* (2009) both announces key references and assists readers to unlock layers of authorial design (the 'why' of fiction instead of translation, included). Virgil's poetry, writes Le Guin (2009: 273), is so

> profoundly musical, its beauty is so intrinsic to the sound and order of the words, that it is essentially untranslatable. Even Dryden, even FitzGerald couldn't capture the magic. But a translator's yearning to identify with the text cannot be repressed. This is what urged me to take some scenes, some hints, some foreshadowings from the epic and make them into a novel – a translation into a different *form* – partial, marginal, but, in intent at least, faithful.

The role of notes is also integral to an understanding of a poetic offering like Balmer's *Ghost Passage* (2022), a collection based on findings at the Bloomberg London Building site between 2010 and 2014. The poems imagine the stories behind fragments of Latin discovered in letters, tiles, and items such as pewter amulets from the excavation (the book's section titles, foregrounding the materials, are telling: 'In Wood', 'Through Clay', 'On Stone (Oxney sonnets)'). Balmer's verse links remnants of Roman London with afterimages in contemporary Britain. A few of the poems were presented in a 2019 reading at the London Mithraeum Bloomberg SPACE,[15] and the subsequent volume, also drawing in other classical material, doubles as a textual extension of the excavation site. Connections of translation and classical reception in a title poem that already indicates to us 'after Procopius (*On the Wars* 8.20 47–58)' are elucidated paratextually: an endnote tells us how the Byzantine historian

> recounts that he learnt this story from British travellers included in a Frankish embassy to the court of Justinian in Byzantium. It is possible that, hearing of an 'Isle of the Dead', Procopius might have confused the Greek for death (*thanatos*) with the Isle of Thanet which he might have seen on Roman maps.
> A tiny carved cameo seal, dating from the third century CE and found on the Thames foreshore, depicts a ghostly Roman rowing boat with four sailors. It is now on display in the Museum of London. (Balmer 2022: 86)

'The Library versus the Lyre', Balmer's (2019) essay on the conception of her 2017 collection *The Paths of Survival*, also dwells on the ways in which classical absences (in this case, that of Aeschylus' long-lost play *Myrmidons*) may fire the imagination. This is because certain effects can be attained only in literary space: 'where scholarship deals in establishing the known, the deductive, poetry seeks to re-enact the complexity, the fluidity of moral systems and beliefs. In addition, where scholarship looks to convince, poetry prefers to stand on moving ground, undermining its own arguments, transgressing its own truths' (Balmer 2019: 77).

With Carson, we witness an armamentarium of performative deployments of paratext that I and others have investigated (Nikolaou 2022b). This is not least since, as she admits, 'I put scholarly projects and so-called creative projects side-by-side in my workspace, and I cross back and forth between them or move sentences back and forth between them, and so cause them to permeate one another' (in McNeilly and Carson 2003: 14). Various metabolisms emerge: in Carson's engagement with Sappho, an introductory text 'On Marks and Lacks' (Carson 2003) outlines a rigorous meditation on the dramas of reading fragmented sources. The process of rendering Sappho appositely proves itself through what empty spaces make possible, or help suggest to a reader:

> Brackets are an aesthetic gesture toward the papyrological event rather than an accurate record of it. I have not used brackets in translating passages, phrases or words whose existence depends on citation by ancient authors, since these are intentionally incomplete. I emphasize the distinction between brackets and no brackets because it will affect your reading experience, if you

---

allow it. Brackets are exciting. Even though you are approaching Sappho in translation, that is no reason you should miss the drama of trying to read a papyrus torn in half or riddled with holes or smaller than a postage stamp – brackets imply a free space of imaginal adventure. (p. xi)

The side-by-side existence of the Sappho textual remnants and Carson's English formations shows how she often re-concentrates both absences and meanings, as when fragment 8,

].ν. ọ .[
] ἀμφ.[
Ἄ]τθι σο.[
]. νέφ[
] [

turns to:

]
]
]Atthis for you
]
]

(Carson 2003: 18–19)

Norma Jeane Baker of Troy (2020), a more recent dramatic work by Carson for the Shed's Griffin Theater in New York in 2019, is another instance of classical versioning where critical language inventively enters the poet-translator's endeavour. As the programme notes online imply,[16] this is a version of Euripides' *Helen*, where the transition from translating to creative speculation is the very theme: 'It is 1964. An office manager has hired one of his stenos to come in at night and type out his translation of Euripides's *Helen*, but his obsession with the recently dead Marilyn Monroe kidnaps the translation.' In what follows, Euripides' intentions are reflected upon, and Marilyn Monroe, although in Los Angeles, is suggested as being 'of Troy'; it happens through multiple framings of translation or anachronisms 'permeating both the text, and those only apparently paratextual, "lesson plans" that are very much part of a performance, and creative construction and intent of *Norma Jeane Baker of Troy*' (Nikolaou 2022b: 125). These interjected, elliptical lesson outlines themselves start with translation of an ancient Greek word (such as 'εἴδωλον', for which Carson (2020: 13) lists: 'image, likeness, simulacrum, replica, proxy, idol') that provides a key to the action preceding or following. A 'case study' may follow that adds suggestive illustration: 'The Russian military now uses

---

[16] As found on the website for The Shed: https://theshed.org/program/4-norma-jeane-baker-of-troy.

decoy armaments of a Euripidean design – lifesize tanks, MiG–31 fighter jets and missile launchers made of inflatable plastic. A hot-air balloon company provides them to the Ministry of Defense' (Carson 2020: 13). Paratextual interjections, therefore, are very much part of the creative structure and recall *Nox* (2010), Carson's autobiographical and experimental translation of Catullus' poem 101, which doubles as a lament for Carson's dead brother. In *Nox*, the telling of painful experiences occurs through the staging of the process of rendering a classical text into English. The book itself is a painstakingly considered artefact, its unfolding, non-numbered pages resembling a draft contained in a box. Typography and design help realize Carson's intentions: right-hand pages present one of the words of the original, facing its dictionary definition on the left-hand page. With *Nox*, we procure meaning through paratextual devices and exegesis; they *themselves* turn into content/text, as situations and sites of translating are in the service of a narrative that fuses literary effort and oblique life writing.

A second edition of *Antigonick* returns us to the practice of poems addressing the reader of classical translations. Only this time, a text such as 'The Task of the Translator of Antigone' is more cognizant of accumulating theory and receptions than Chapman's 'To the Reader of *Homer's Iliad*'. The space normally dedicated to a paratext transforms into poetic delivery of Carson's personal thoughts on translations of the play. A comparable case is 'I Wish I Were Two Dogs Then I Could Play with Me (Translator's Note on Euripides' *Bakkhai*)' – which opens Carson's (Euripides 2017) version. These six pages of three-line stanzas are a self-aware introduction of the figure of Dionysus that dominates the drama. Critical notes metastasize into verse that is populated by scenes of the play's reception: with mentions of Stephen Hawking, Sigmund Freud, and Bertolt Brecht helping us to perceive how Euripides has been read across time. We are reminded, inside the brackets featured in the poem's title, that this still serves as a 'translator's note', both resisting typical demands – and forms – of criticism and commentary for classical translation, and uniquely suited to this *Bakkhai*.

The conventions of paratext also participate poignantly in mirroring and amplifying the spirit of the classical author in *After Fame: The Epigrams of Martial* (2020) by Sam Riviere, who selects only the first book in what his publisher terms 'a discursive rendering'; a later clarification on Faber's website is even more suggestive of textual ambiguity as the *raison d'être* for Riviere's book: '[p]itched between translation and new writing, *After Fame* challenges the integrity of both categories, dramatising the obscurity of its source, refrain-ing from easy equivalences, while insisting on its contemporary relevance'.[17]

---

[17] It forms the latter part of the summary for the publication, as found here: www.faber.co.uk/product/9780571356935-after-fame/.

The varied practising of forms of translation across a Martial possessed by and possessing Riviere reflects 'with subtlety and seriousness on how an ancient author may pitch meaning across time or be recuperated as a creative resource', as Nisbet (2021: 225) has argued. Riviere deploys a panoply of possible interpenetrations of translation and paratext, so that *After Fame*'s creativity coincides with inventive appropriations of modes of classical reception: the modern poet often deliberates on his experiments with Google Translate in reproducing a Martialic tone. Machine translation 'struggles with Latin', as Riviere further points out in an interview; consequently, the writing process 'began in that margin of error – attempting to bridge the gap between whatever the program had spat out, and something that felt like a poem to me. These became less and less obviously related to the original poems as I went on' (in Riding 2020). What is more, the poet-translator's adopted methods, as would be recorded in a paratext, radically invade some of the sections into which Riviere divides Book 1. While in the first one, more 'regular' versioning appears to take place, textual footnotes crop up soon after 'Work and Leisure' (Riviere 2020: 39–57) begins. Nisbet (2021: 224) has noted how Riviere's 'cover' of 1.52 turns to a pretext for an elaborate commentary on the nature of impersonation and unauthorized copying. The poet himself has pointed out that 'all writing has elements of plagiarism – or recycling and repurposing – much more than we usually admit' (Riding 2020). Across *After Fame* he sees fit to play around

> with the tropes of scholarly editions of ancient texts – notes, corrections, addenda, suppositions, speculations, editorial interventions . . . I was reading quite a lot about Martial as I started to get more immersed in the 'translation' process, if that's what it was, so the book is perhaps best viewed as a record of reading the poems, in the sort of multifarious way you have to when the original text isn't legible (I have no Latin to speak of). (Riding 2020)

The process of poet understanding poet is further textualized, sometimes by bringing line-by-line exegesis into play. 'Law and Rhetoric' (Riviere 2020: 85–8), a section that overwrites Martial 1.81–98, doubles as a parody of copyright pages. The previous section, titled 'Friendship, Family, Marriage' (59–83) also embeds glimpses of influences or feedback on the work, accruals of drafts made visible as the modern poet struggles with the material – while in place of 1.71, Riviere (2020: 67) reflects on a period of difficulty in his own marriage syncing with his reading *Contempt* by Alberto Moravia, 'about a man who suspects that his wife no longer loves him'. In this sense, Riviere's personal experience as he progresses through Moravia's first chapters is 'on a kind of parallel track to the drama of the novel'. The reading and translating 'I' is repetitively biographized, and only in the titular, closing section do we return to versioned Martial. However, as Nesbit (2021:

224–5) points out, 'even this soothing surface is cover for fevered ego-narration unfolding in the footnotes, where Martial/Riviere makes elaborate imaginary war upon a shadowy "adversary". This "rival archivist" threatens to out-trend him and to elide the poet/translator's claims to cultural edginess.'

As in Carson's *Nox*, we take note of interplays of draft or 'treatments' and published text, intricate dualities of paratext as metatext. What is more, there is overlap between some of these metatexts and metadiscourse (see Batchelor 2018: 151), which in the case of translation necessarily involves discussions about the very phenomenon of translating. It becomes clearer that such invent-ive use of paratextual space locates and installs a multiplicity of voices and interpretations inside the creative classical translation, one that can now accom-plish a polyphonic staging of readings past and present.

In combination with preceding sections, our attention to literary transform-ations of translators' commentary and statements here further confirms creative imperatives behind, and the variety of formations attempted through a starting point of, classical translation. Such paratexts carry weight and show frequency that merits consistent discussion, as in this Element.

There is, then, a poetics of translation synchronizing with intentions, accents, and designs particular to the classics or more habitually encountered in this realm than in customary cases of a poet inventively translating one of their contemporaries. Certain modes pertaining to rereading, retranslation, re-creation, and recontextualizing as explored throughout this Element also pre-sent a case for consistent assimilation of their specific aspirations in subsequent research – whether in classical reception or literary, cultural, and translations studies – as well as in creative writing practices and exercises.

References

Adamitis, J. & Gamel, M.-K. (2013). Theaters of War. In D. Lateiner, B. K. Gold, & J. Perkins, eds., *Roman Literature, Gender and Reception: Domina Illustris*. New York: Routledge, pp. 284–302.

Almond, M. (2009). Horace on Teesside. In S. J. Harrison, ed., *Living Classics: Greece and Rome in Contemporary Poetry in English*. Oxford: Oxford University Press, pp. 19–42.

'Antigone' (2022). *Australian Arts Review (Theatre)*, 26 May. https://artsre view.com.au/antigone-2/.

Armitage, S. (2000). *Mister Heracles: After Euripides*. London: Faber and Faber.

Armitage, S. (2008). Introduction. In *The Odyssey: A Dramatic Retelling of Homer's Epic*. New York: W. W. Norton & Company, pp. v–vi.

Armitage, S. (2016). *Still*. London: Enitharmon.

Arnold, M. ([1809] 1960). On Translating Homer. In *The Complete Prose Works of Matthew Arnold, Vol. 1: On the Classical Tradition*, ed. R. H. Super. Ann Arbor: University of Michigan Press, pp. 97–216.

Arnold, M. ([1849] 2019). Fragment of an 'Antigone'. In *Poetical Works*. Frankfurt: Outlook, pp. 204–6.

Asimakoulas, D. (2019). *Rewriting Humour in Comic Books: Cultural Transfer and Translation of Aristophanic Adaptations*. Palgrave Studies in Translating and Interpreting. Cham: Palgrave Macmillan.

Athanassakis, A. N. (ed. & trans.) (1976). *The Homeric Hymns*. Baltimore, MD: Johns Hopkins University Press.

Atwood, M. (2005). *The Penelopiad: The Myth of Penelope and Odysseus*. Canongate Myths. Edinburgh: Canongate.

Avianus (1993). *The Fables of Avianus*, trans. D. R. Slavitt. Baltimore, MD: Johns Hopkins University Press.

Bainbridge, C. (2005). The War in Heaven. *The Guardian*, October 8. www. theguardian.com/books/2005/oct/08/poetry.homer.

Balmer, J. (2004a). *Chasing Catullus: Poems, Translations and Transgressions*. Newcastle upon Tyne: Bloodaxe Books.

Balmer, J. (2004b). *Catullus: Poems of Love and Hate*, trans. J. Balmer. Newcastle upon Tyne: Bloodaxe Books.

Balmer, J. (2005). The Word for Sorrow: A Work Begins Its Progress. *Modern Poetry in Translation* 3(3), 60–8.

Balmer. J. (2009). *The Word for Sorrow*. Cambridge: Salt.

Balmer, J. (2013). *Piecing Together the Fragments: Translating Classical Verse, Creating Contemporary Poetry.* Classical Presences. Oxford: Oxford University Press.

Balmer, J. (2017a). *Letting Go: Thirty Mourning Sonnets and Two Poems.* Mayfield: Agenda Editions.

Balmer, J. (2017b). *The Paths of Survival.* Bristol: Shearsman Books.

Balmer, J. (2019). The Library versus the Lyre: *The Paths of Survival* and the Poetry of Textual History. *Synthesis: An Anglophone Journal of Comparative Literary Studies* 12 ('Recomposed: Anglophone Presences of Classical Literature'), 76–95.

Balmer, J. (2022). *Ghost Passage.* Swindon: Shearsman Books.

Barker, P. (2018). *The Silence of the Girls.* London: Hamish Hamilton.

Bartsch, S. (2020). Introduction to the Poem. In Vergil, *The Aeneid.* London: Profile Books, pp. xv–xliii.

Bassnett, S. (2019). On Rereading Homer's *Iliad* in the Twenty-First Century. *Synthesis: An Anglophone Journal of Comparative Literary Studies* 12 ('Recomposed: Anglophone Presences of Classical Literature'), 96–102.

Bassnett, S. (2022). Translation, Transcreation, Transgression. In L. Jansen, ed., *Anne Carson/Antiquity.* Bloomsbury Studies in Classical Reception. London: Bloomsbury Academic, pp. 237–50.

Batchelor, K. (2018). *Translation and Paratexts.* Translation Theories Explained. London: Routledge.

Bergin, T. (2018). Hughes As Translator. In T. Gifford, ed., *Ted Hughes in Context.* Cambridge: Cambridge University Press, pp. 72–81.

Blakesley, M. (2018). Tony Harrison the Translator: 'Life's a Performance. Either Join in / Lightheartedly, or Thole the Pain'. *English Studies* 99(1), 51–66.

Boland, E. (ed. & trans.) (2004). *After Every War: Twentieth-Century Women Poets.* Princeton, NJ: Princeton University Press.

Boland, E. (2011). Translating the Underworld. In *A Journey with Two Maps: Becoming a Woman Poet.* New York: W. W. Norton, pp. 77–97.

Boland, E. (2012). Afterword. In A. Oswald, *Memorial.* New York: Farrar, Straus and Giroux, pp. 83–90.

Borges, J. L. (1999). The Homeric Versions. In E. Weinberger, ed., *Selected Non-fictions*, trans. E. Allen, S. J. Levine, & E. Weinberger. New York: Viking, pp. 69–74.

Braund, S. (2018). Virgil after Vietnam. In S. Braund & Z. Martirosova Torlone, eds., *Virgil and His Translators.* Classical Presences. Oxford: Oxford University Press, pp. 107–23.

Brower, R. A. (1947). Seven Agamemnons. *Journal of the History of Ideas* 8(4), 383–405.

Brower, R. A. (1974). *Mirror on Mirror: Translation, Limitation, Parody.* Studies in Comparative Literature 33. Cambridge, MA: Harvard University Press.

Bruno, R. & Carson, A. (2021). *Euripides. The Trojan Women: A Comic.* New York: New Directions.

Burke, P. (1998). *The European Renaissance: Centres and Peripheries.* Oxford: Blackwell.

Burkitt, K. (2007). Imperial Reflections: The Post-Colonial Verse-Novel as Post-Epic. In L. Hardwick & C. Gillespie, eds., *Classics in Post-Colonial Worlds.* Classical Presences. Oxford: Oxford University Press, pp. 157–69.

Burt, S. (2020). Imitator's Note. In *After Callimachus: Poems,* foreword M. Payne. The Lockert Library of Poetry in Translation. Princeton, NJ: Princeton University Press, pp. xxii–xxv.

Byron, L. (1819). *Don Juan.* London: printed by Thomas Davison, Whitefriars.

Callimachus (1988). *Hymns, Epigrams, Select Fragments,* trans. S. Lombardo & D. Rayor. Baltimore, MD: Johns Hopkins University Press.

Carson, A. (1998). *Autobiography of Red.* New York: Knopf.

Carson, A. (2003). *If Not, Winter: Fragments of Sappho.* New York: Knopf.

Carson, A. (2006). 'Why I Wrote Two Plays about Phaidra'. In *Grief Lessons: Four Plays by Euripides.* New York: New York Review Books Classics, pp. 309–12.

Carson, A. (2009). *An Oresteia: Agamemnon by Aiskhylos; Elektra by Sophokles; Orestes by Euripides.* New York: Faber and Faber.

Carson, A. (2010). *Nox.* New York: New Directions.

Carson, A. (2013). *Red Doc.* New York: Knopf.

Carson, A. (2015). The Task of the Translator of Antigone. In *Antigonick.* New York: New Directions, pp. 3–6.

Carson, A. (2017). 'I Wish I Were Two Dogs Then I Could Play with Me'. In Euripides, *Bakkhai: A New Version by Anne Carson.* New York: New Directions, pp. 7–12.

Carson, A. (2020). *Norma Jeane Baker of Troy.* New York: New Directions.

Cather, W. (1918). *My Ántonia.* Boston, MA: Houghton Mifflin.

Chang, D. (2011). Democracy at War: Antigone: Insurgency in Toronto. In E. B. Mee & Helene P. Foley, eds., *Antigone on the Contemporary World Stage.* Classical Presences. Oxford: Oxford University Press, pp. 267–85.

Chapman, G. (2005). To the Reader of *Homer's Iliad.* In B. Blaisdell, ed., *Elizabethan Poetry: An Anthology.* Mineola, NY: Dover Publications, pp. 24–8.

Console, C. (2011). *The Odicy.* Richmond, CA: Omnidawn.

Constantine, P. (trans.). (2001). *Hölderlin's Sophocles: Oedipus and Antigone.* Tarset: Bloodaxe.

Constantine, P. (2011). Service Abroad: *Hölderlin,* Poet-Translator. A Lecture. *Translation and Literature* 20(1), 79–97.

Cole, E. (2020). The Wooster Group's *To You, The Birdie!* In *Postdramatic Tragedies*. Classical Presences. Oxford: Oxford University Press, pp. 143–75.

Cox, F. (2018). *Ovid's Presence in Contemporary Women's Writing: Strange Monsters*. Classical Presences. Oxford: Oxford University Press.

Davenport, G. (trans.) (1995). *7 Greeks*. New York: New Directions.

Demanski, L. (2021). An Aeneas Divided. *The University of Chicago Magazine* 113(2), 27–31.

Dryden, J. (1992). On Translation. In R. Schulte & J. Biguenet, eds., *Theories of Translation: An Anthology of Essays from Dryden to Derrida*. Chicago, IL: University of Chicago Press, pp. 17–31.

Doolitle, H. (1986). Translations 1915–1920. In L. L. Martz, ed., *Collected Poems 1912–1944*. New York: New Directions.

duBois, P. (2015). Queer Sappho. In *Sappho*. London: I. B. Tauris, pp. 155–74.

Duggan, G. & Noto, P. (2012). *The Infinite Horizon*. Portland, OR: Image Comics.

Eccleston, S.-M. (2019). Cyrus Console's *The Odicy* and Epic Ecology. *Classical Receptions Journal* 11(1), 23–43.

Eco, U. (2004). *Mouse or Rat? Translation As Negotiation*. London: Weidenfeld & Nicolson.

Euripides (2017). *Bakkhai: A New Version by Anne Carson*. New York: New Directions.

Ellison, R. (1952). *Invisible Man*. New York: Random House.

Ellison, R. (2010). *Three Days Before the Shooting . . .*. New York: Random House.

Fagles, R. (2001). Translator's Postscript. In Homer, *The Odyssey*. London: Penguin Books, pp. 419–26.

Fagles, R. (2006). Postscript. In Virgil, *The Aeneid*. New York: Viking Penguin, pp. 389–405.

Fitzgerald, R. (1952). Heroic Poems in English. *The Kenyon Review* 14(4), 698–706.

Fitzgerald, R. (1981). Postscript: Virgil's *The Aeneid*. In Virgil, *The Aeneid*. New York: Random House, pp. 412–14.

Frost, R. (1914). *North of Boston*. London: David Nutt.

Genette, G. (1997). *Paratexts: Thresholds of Interpretation*, trans. J. E. Lewin. Cambridge: Cambridge University Press.

Gibbs, J. (2007). Antigone and Her African Sisters: West African Versions of a Greek Original. In L. Hardwick & C. Gillespie, eds., *Classics in Post-Colonial Worlds*. Classical Presences. Oxford: Oxford University Press, pp. 54–71.

Gifford, T. (ed.) (2018). *Ted Hughes in Context*. Cambridge: Cambridge University Press.

Gillespie, S. (2011). *English Translation and Classical Reception: Towards a New Literary History.* Malden, MA: Wiley-Blackwell.

Gillespie, S. (2021). John Polwhele's Horatian Translations. *Translation and Literature* 30(1), 30–51.

Glück, L. (1996). *Meadowlands.* New York: The Ecco Press.

Graves, R. (trans.) (1959). *The Anger of Achilles. Homer's* Iliad. Illustrations by D. Searle. New York: Doubleday & Company.

Green, P. (2012). Homer Now. *The New Republic*, June 7. https://newrepublic .com/article/103920/homer-the-iliad-translations.

Greenwood, E. (2009). Sounding Out Homer: Christopher Logue's Acoustic Homer. *Oral Tradition* 24(2), 503–18.

Hadas, R. (2018). *Poems for Camilla.* Evansville, IN: Measure Press.

Hallett, J. P. (2016). Greek (and Roman) Ways and Thoroughfares: The Routing of Edith Hamilton's Classical Antiquity. In R. Wyles & E. Hall, eds., *Women Classical Scholars: Unsealing the Fountain from the Renaissance to Jacqueline de Romilly.* Classical Presences. Oxford: Oxford University Press, pp. 216–42.

Hamilton, E. (1930). *The Greek Way.* New York: W. W. Norton.

Hamilton, E. (1964). *The Ever Present Past.* New York: W. W. Norton.

Hardwick, L. (2000). Greek Drama at the End of the Twentieth Century: Cultural Renaissance or Performative Outrage? The Open University (Classical Receptions in Drama and Poetry in English from c.1970–2005). www.open.ac.uk/arts/research/greekplays/publications/essays/hardwick-greek-drama-20th-century.

Hardwick, L. (2003). *Reception Studies.* Greece and Rome: New Surveys in the Classics, 33. Oxford: Oxford University Press.

Hardwick, L. (2007). Shades of Multi-Lingualism and Multi-Vocalism in Modern Performances of Greek Tragedy in Post-Colonial Contexts. In L. Hardwick & C. Gillespie, eds., *Classics in Post-Colonial Worlds.* Classical Presences. Oxford: Oxford University Press, pp. 305–28.

Hardwick, L. (2011). Fuzzy Connections: Classical Texts and Modern Poetry in English. In J. Parker & T. Matthews, eds., *Tradition, Translation, Trauma: The Classic and the Modern.* Classical Presences. Oxford: Oxford University Press, pp. 39–60.

Hardwick, L. & Gillespie, C. (eds.). (2007). *Classics in Post-Colonial Worlds.* Classical Presences. Oxford: Oxford University Press.

Harrison, S. J. (2009). Introduction: The Return of Classics. In S. J. Harrison, ed., *Living Classics: Greece and Rome in Contemporary Poetry in English.* Oxford: Oxford University Press, pp. 1–16.

Harrison, T. (1981). *U.S. Martial.* Newcastle: Bloodaxe Books.

Harrison, T. (2005). Bitter Tears. *The Guardian*, March 19. www.theguardian.com/
stage/2005/mar/19/theatre.classics.

Heaney, C. & Hollis, M. (2016). Note on the Text. In S. Heaney *Aeneid: Book
VI*. London: Faber and Faber, pp. 51–3.

Heaney, S. (1991). Choruses from 'The Cure' at Troy: A Version of Sophocles'
'Philoctetes'. *Arion: A Journal of Humanities and the Classics*. Third Series,
1(2), 131–8.

Heaney, S. (2001a). Horace and the Thunder. *The Irish Times*, 17 November.

Heaney, S. (2001b). *Electric Light*. London: Faber and Faber.

Heaney, S. (2004a). *Anything Can Happen: A Poem and Essay by Seamus
Heaney with Translations in Support of Art for Amnesty*. Dublin:
Townhouse.

Heaney, S. (2004b). *The Burial at Thebes: Sophocles'* Antigone *translated by
Seamus Heaney*. London: Faber and Faber.

Heaney, S. (2005). 'Me' as in 'Metre': On Translating Antigone. In. J. Dillon &
S. E. Wilmer, eds., *Rebel Women: Staging Ancient Greek Drama Today*.
London: Methuen, pp. 166–73.

Heaney, S. (2009). Title Deeds: Translating a Classic. In S. J. Harrison, ed.,
Living Classics: Greece and Rome in Contemporary Poetry in English.
Oxford: Oxford University Press, pp. 122–39.

Heaney, S. (2010). Route 110. In *Human Chain*. London: Faber and Faber, pp.
48–59.

Heaney, S. (2016). Translator's Note. In *Aeneid: Book VI*. London: Faber and
Faber, pp. vii–ix.

Heaney, S. & Hass, R. (2000). *Sounding Lines: The Art of Translating Poetry*.
Doreen B. Townsend Center for the Humanities Occasional Papers, 20.
Berkeley, CA: University of California Press.

Heaney, S. & O'Driscoll, D. (2003). Seamus Heaney with Dennis O'Driscoll.
Lannan Foundation. https://lannan.org/events/seamus-heaney-with-dennis-
odriscoll.

Hofmann, M. & Lasdun, J. (eds.) (1996). *After Ovid: New Metamorphoses*.
New York: Noonday.

Homer (1860). *The Iliad of Homer*, trans. W. Cowper, ed. R. Southey. New York:
D. Appleton.

Homer ([1715] 1906). Pope's Iliad of Homer, ed. A. J. Church. London:
Cassell.

Homer (1946). *The Odyssey*, trans. E. V. Rieu. Penguin Classics 1. London:
Penguin Books.

Homer (1950). *The Iliad*, trans. E. V. Rieu. London: Penguin Books.

Homer (1951). *The Iliad*, trans. R. Lattimore. Chicago, IL: University of Chicago Press.

Homer (1961). *Homer's Odyssey*, trans. R. Fitzgerald, ed. G. S. Kirk. New York: Farrar, Straus and Giroux.

Homer (1974). *The Iliad*, trans. R. Fitzgerald. New York: Doubleday.

Homer (1990). *The Iliad*, trans. R. Fagles. New York: Penguin.

Homer (1996). *The Odyssey*, trans. R. Fagles. New York: Penguin.

Homer (1997). *The Iliad*, trans. S. Lombardo, ed. S. Murnaghan. Indianapolis, IN: Hackett Publishing.

Homer (2011). *Iliad*, trans. S. Mitchell. New York: Free Press.

Homer (2023). *The Iliad*, trans. E. Wilson. New York: W. W. Norton.

Homerus & West, M. (1998). *Volumen I: Rhapsodiae I–XII.* Bibliotheca scriptorum Graecorum et Romanorum Teubneriana. Stuttgart: B. G. Teubner.

Hooper, R. (1888). Introduction. In *The Iliads of Homer*, trans. G. Chapman. London: John Russell Smith, pp. x–lxi.

Hope, D. & Roberts, M. (2022). What Makes Music Sound American? In *America*. CD Recording: Deutsche Grammophon, pp. 7–13.

Hughes, T. (1972). *Crow: From the Life and Songs of the Crow*. London: Faber and Faber.

Hughes, T. (1983). *Seneca's Oedipus, adapted by Ted Hughes*. London: Faber and Faber.

Hughes, T. (1997). *Tales from Ovid: Twenty-Four Passages from the 'Metamorphoses'*. London: Faber and Faber.

Hughes, T. (1999). *Alcestis: In a Version by Ted Hughes*. London: Faber and Faber.

Ioannidou, E. (2017). *Greek Fragments in Postmodern Frames: Rewriting Tragedy 1970–2005*. Classical Presences. Oxford: Oxford University Press.

Jakovljevic, B. (2010). Wooster Baroque. *TDR: The Drama Review* 54 (3), 87–122.

Jay, P. & Lewis, C. (eds.) (1996). *Sappho through English Poetry*. London: Anvil Press Poetry.

Jerome (2004). Letter to Pammachius, trans. K. Davies. In L. Venuti, ed., *The Translation Studies Reader*, 2nd ed. London: Routledge, pp. 21–30.

Jusdanis, G. (2017). Black Odysseus: An Elegy. *Arcade: Literature, the Humanities and the World*. https://arcade.stanford.edu/blogs/black-odysseus-elegy.

Kazantzakis, N. ([1938] 1958). *The Odyssey: A Modern Sequel*, trans. K. Friar. New York: Simon & Schuster.

Kim, S. (2021). Riot Antigone: After Sophocles' Antigone. In M. Powers, ed., *Reclaiming Greek Drama for Diverse Audiences: An Anthology of Adaptations and Interviews*. London: Routledge, pp. 212–48.

Köhler, B. (2007). *Niemands Frau*. Berlin: Suhrkamp Verlag.

Kozak, L. & Hickman, M. (eds.) (2019). *The Classics in Modernist Translation*. London: Bloomsbury Academic.

Lamb, C. (1808). *The Adventures of Ulysses*. London: Printed by T. Davison for the Juvenile Library.

Leezenberg, M. (2007). From the Peloponnesian War to the Iraq War: A Post-Liberal Reading of Greek Tragedy. In L. Hardwick & C. Gillespie, eds., *Classics in Post-Colonial Worlds*. Classical Presences. Oxford: Oxford University Press, pp. 265–85.

Lefevere, A. (1975). *Translating Poetry: Seven Strategies and a Blueprint*. Assen: Van Gorcum.

Lefevere, A. & Bassnett, S. (1998). Introduction: Where Are We in Translation Studies? In S. Bassnett & A. Lefevere, eds., *Constructing Cultures: Essays in Literary Translation*. Topics in Translation 11. Clevedon: Multilingual Matters, pp. 1–11.

Le Guin, U. K. (2009). Afterword. In *Lavinia*. Boston, MA: Mariner Books, pp. 273–9.

Levine, J. S. (1984). Translation As (Sub)Version: On Translating *Infante's Inferno*. *SubStance* 13(1), 85–94.

Levitan, M. & Lombardo, S. (eds.) (2022). *The* Dionysiaca *of Nonnus of Panopolis: A Group Translation*. Ann Arbor: University of Michigan Press.

Liebregts, P. (2019). *Translations of Greek Tragedy in the Work of Ezra Pound*. London: Bloomsbury.

Liveley, G. (2019). 'After His Wine-Dark Sea': H.D. in Homer. In F. Cox & E. Theodorakopoulos, eds., *Homer's Daughters: Women's Responses to Homer in the Twentieth Century and Beyond*. Classical Presences. Oxford: Oxford University Press, pp. 21–38.

Logue, C. (1962). *Patrocleia: Book XVI of Homer's* Iliad *adapted by Christopher Logue*. London: Scorpion Press.

Logue, C. (1981). *Ode to the Dodo: Poems 1953–1978*. London: Jonathan Cape.

Logue, C. (1991). *Kings: An Account of Books 1 and 2 of Homer's* Iliad. New York: Farrar, Straus and Giroux.

Logue, C. (1995). *The Husbands: An Account of Books 3 and 4 of Homer's* Iliad. New York: Farrar, Straus and Giroux.

Logue, C. (1996). A Chorus from Antigone. In *Selected Poems*, ed. C. Reid. London: Faber and Faber, pp. 6–7.

Logue, C. (2003). *All Day Permanent Red: The First Battle Scenes of Homer's Iliad Rewritten*. New York: Farrar, Straus and Giroux.

Logue, C. (2005). *Cold Calls: War Music Continued*. London: Faber and Faber.

Logue, C. (2015). *War Music: An Account of Homer's Iliad*, ed. C. Reid. London: Faber and Faber.

Lombardo, S. (2001). Homer's Light: The Odyssey Koan. Paper presented at Hampshire College (April). https://kansaszencenter.org/wp-content/uploads/2020/07/Homers-Light-The-Odyssey-Koan.pdf.

Longley, M. (1994). Ceasefire. *The Irish Times*, 3 September.

Lowell, R. ([1961] 1990). *Imitations*. New York: Farrar, Straus and Giroux.

Machacek, G. (2011). *Milton and Homer: 'Written to Aftertimes'*. Pittsburgh: Duquesne University Press.

Macintosh, F. (2016). Conquering England: Ireland and Greek Tragedy. In B. van Zyl Smit, ed., *A Handbook to the Reception of Greek Drama*. Hoboken, NJ: John Wiley and Sons, pp. 323–36.

Mack, P. & North, J. (eds.) (2015). Introduction. In *The Afterlife of Ovid*. London: Institute of Classical Studies, School of Advanced Study, University of London, pp. vii–xi.

Mahon, D. (2022). The *Adaptations 1975–2020*. Loughcrew: The Gallery Press.

Malmkjær, K. (2020). *Translation and Creativity*. London: Routledge.

Malouf, D. (2009). *Ransom*. New York: Random House.

Martindale, C. (1993). *Redeeming the Text: Latin Poetry and the Hermeneutics of Reception*. Cambridge: Cambridge University Press.

Mason, H. A. (1969). Creative Translation: Ezra Pound's Women of Trachis. *The Cambridge Quarterly* 4(3), 244–72.

Mason, Z. (2018). *Metamorphica*. New York: Farrar, Straus and Giroux.

Matthias, J. (2016). Camilla of the Volscians. In *Complayntes for Doctor Neuro and Other Poems*. Bristol: Shearsman Books, pp. 50–4.

Mazzucchelli, D. (2009). *Asterios Polyp*. New York: Pantheon.

McClatchy, J. D. (ed.) (2002). *The Odes: New Translations by Contemporary Poets*. Princeton, NJ: Princeton University Press.

McConnell, J. (2013). *Black Odysseys: The Homeric* Odyssey *in the African Diaspora since 1939*. Classical Presences. Oxford: Oxford University Press.

McNeilly, K. & Carson, A. (2003). Gifts and Questions: An Interview with Anne Carson. *Canadian Literature* 176, 12–25.

Meineck, P. (2014). 'The Thorniest Problem and the Greatest Opportunity': Directors on Directing the Greek chorus. In R. Gagné & M. Govers Hopman, eds., *Choral Mediations in Greek Tragedy*. Cambridge: Cambridge University Press, pp. 352–83.

Meineck, P. (2016). Greek Drama in North America. In B. van Zyl Smit, ed., *A Handbook to the Reception of Greek Drama.* Hoboken, NJ: John Wiley and Sons, pp. 173–98.

Minier, M. (2013). Definitions, Dyads, Triads and Other Points of Connection in Translation and Adaptation Discourse. In K. Krebs, ed., *Translation and Adaptation in Theatre and Film.* New York: Routledge, pp. 13–31.

Moul, V. (2010). *Jonson, Horace and the Classical Tradition.* Cambridge: Cambridge University Press.

Mueller, M. (2021). Sappho and Sexuality. In P. J. Finglass & A. Kelly, eds., *The Cambridge Companion to Sappho.* Cambridge Companions to Literature. Cambridge: Cambridge University Press, pp. 36–52.

Murnaghan, S. (1997). Introduction. In Homer, *The Iliad*, trans. S. Lombardo. Indianapolis, IN: Hackett Publishing, pp. xlix–lvii.

Nikolaou, P. (2017). 'The *Iliad* Suits You': Christopher Logue's Homer – from *Patrocleia* (1962) to the Posthumous Edition of *War Music.* In *The Return of Pytheas: Scenes from British and Greek Poetry in Dialogue.* Bristol: Shearsman Books, pp. 17–40.

Nikolaou, P. (2019). Introduction: Angloclassical? *Synthesis: An Anglophone Journal of Comparative Literary Studies* 12 ('Recomposed: Anglophone Presences of Classical Literature'), 1–20.

Nikolaou, P. (2020). *Poems for Camilla* by Rachel Hadas. *The Hopkins Review* 13(2), 309–13.

Nikolaou, P. (2022a). An Aeneid in New York. *Literary Matters* 14(2). www .literarymatters.org/14-2-an-aeneid-in-new-york-rachel-hadas-interviewed-by-paschalis-nikolaou/.

Nikolaou, P. (2022b). The Paratextual Cosmos. In L. Jansen, ed., *Anne Carson/ Antiquity.* Bloomsbury Studies in Classical Reception. London: Bloomsbury Academic, pp. 119–33.

Nims, J. F. (1971). *Sappho to Valéry: Poems in Translation.* Princeton, NJ: Princeton University Press.

Nisbet, G. (2021). *Epigrams of Martial* by Sam Riviere. *Translation and Literature* 30(2), 219–26.

Nonnos (1940–2). *Dionysiaca*, trans. W. H. D. Rouse. 3 vols. Loeb Classical Library. Cambridge, MA: Harvard University Press.

'On Translating Nonnus' (2022). In M. Levitan & S. Lombardo, eds., *The Dionysiaca of Nonnus of Panopolis: A Group Translation.* Ann Arbor: University of Michigan Press, pp. 725–52.

Nosbaum, J. (2006). Versions from the *Aeneid* and the *Iliad.* Modern Poetry in Translation, Series 3, No. 5, 122–5.

O'Sullivan, C. (2009). Censoring These 'Racy Morsels of the Vernacular': Loss and Gain in Translations of Apuleius and Catullus. In M. E. ní Chuilleanáin, C. Ó Cuilleanáin, & D. Parris, eds., *Translation and Censorship: Arts of Interference*. Dublin: Four Courts Press, pp. 76–92.

Oswald, A. (2011). *Memorial*. London: Faber and Faber.

Oswald, A. (2016). Tithonus. In *Falling Awake*. London: Jonathan Cape, pp. 43–81.

Oswald, A. (2019). *Nobody: A Hymn to the Sea*. London: Jonathan Cape.

Parker, M. (2019). Speaking Truth to Power: Seamus Heaney's *The Burial at Thebes* and the Poetry of Redress. In S. J. Harrison, F. Macintosh, & H. Eastman, eds., *Seamus Heaney and the Classics: Bann Valley Muses*. Classical Presences. Oxford: Oxford University Press, pp. 98–120.

Paterson, D. (2006). Fourteen Notes on the Version. In *Orpheus: A Version of Rilke's* Die Sonette an Orpheus. London: Faber and Faber, pp. 73–84.

Paul, G. (2019). Excavations in Homer: Speculative Archaeologies in Alice Oswald's and Barbara Köhler's Responses to the *Iliad* and the *Odyssey*. In F. Cox & E. Theodorakopoulos, eds., *Homer's Daughters: Women's Responses to Homer in the Twentieth Century and Beyond*. Classical Presences. Oxford: Oxford University Press, pp. 143–60.

Payne, M. (2020). Foreword. In S. Burt, *After Callimachus: Poems*. The Lockert Library of Poetry in Translation. Princeton, NJ: Princeton University Press, pp. xi–xxi.

Pope, A. (1956). *The Correspondence of Alexander Pope, Vol. 1: 1704–1718*, ed. G. Sherburn. Oxford: Oxford University Press.

Pound, E. (1919). Homage to Sextus Propertius. In *Quia Pauper Amavi*. London: The Egoist, pp. 32–51.

Pound, E. (2003). *The Pisan Cantos*, ed. R. Sieburth. New York: New Directions.

Power, W. (2005). *The Seven*. Musical Play, dir. Jo Bonney, chor. Bill T. Jones.

Powers, M. (ed.) (2020). *Diversifying Greek Tragedy on the Contemporary US Stage: An Anthology of Adaptations and Interviews*. Classical Presences. Oxford: Oxford University Press.

Powers, M. (ed.) (2021). *Reclaiming Greek Drama for Diverse Audiences: An Anthology of Adaptions and Interviews*. London: Routledge.

Prins, Y. (2016). What Is Historical Poetics? *Modern Language Quarterly* 77(1), 13–40.

Ranger, H. (2019). 'Reader, I Married Him/Her': Ali Smith, Ovid, and Queer Translation. *Classical Receptions Journal* 11(3), 231–55.

Rayor, D. J. (1990). Translating Fragments. *Translation Review* 32–33(1), 15–18.

Rayor, D. J. (2016). Reimagining the Fragments of Sappho through Translation. In A. Bierl & A. Lardinois, eds., *The Newest Sappho: P. Sapph. Obbink and P. GC inv. 105, Frs. 1-4: Studies in Archaic and Classical Greek Song*, vol. 2. Leiden: Brill, pp. 396–412.

Rayor, D. J. (2019). Valuing Classical Translations for Outreach, Diversity, and Art. *Society for Classical Studies Blog*, 31 January. https://classicalstudies .org/scs-blog/diane-rayor/blog-valuing-classical-translations-outreach-diver sity-and-art.

Rees, R. (2018). Hughes and the Classics. In T. Gifford, ed., *Ted Hughes in Context*. Cambridge: Cambridge University Press, pp. 123–32.

Reid, C. (2015). Editor's Note. In C. Logue, *War Music: An Account of Homer's Iliad*. London: Faber and Faber, pp. 299–302.

Reynolds, M. (2011). *The Poetry of Translation: From Chaucer and Petrarch to Homer and Logue*. Oxford: Oxford University Press.

Riding, J. (2020). Sam Riviere on Martial, Authenticity and Stealing. *The London Magazine*, April 6. www.thelondonmagazine.org/interview-sam-riv iere-on-martial-authenticity-and-stealing/.

Riding, L. (1937). *A Trojan Ending*. London: Constable.

Riviere, S. (2020). *After Fame: The Epigrams of Martial*. London: Faber and Faber

Robinson, D. (ed.) (2002). *Western Translation Theory from Herodotus to Nietzsche*. London: Routledge.

Robinson, M. (2004). *Gilead*. New York: Farrar, Straus and Giroux.

Roche, A. (2020). Hiberno-Greek Rebel Women: Seamus Heaney's Antigone and the Hecuba of Frank McGuinness and Marina Carr. In P. Nikolaou, ed., *Encounters in Greek and Irish Literature: Creativity, Translations and Critical Perspectives*. Lady Stephenson Library, Newcastle upon Tyne: Cambridge Scholars Publishing, pp. 12–33.

Rolon, K. Grazide, M., Williams, N. et. al. (2021). Interview with Seonjae Kim. In M. Powers, ed., *Reclaiming Greek Drama for Diverse Audiences: An Anthology of Adaptations and Interviews*. London: Routledge, pp.249–55.

Roth, P. (1998). *I Married a Communist*. Boston, MA: Houghton Mifflin.

Roth, P. (2000). *The Human Stain*. New York: Houghton Mifflin.

Roynon, T. (2021). *The Classical Tradition in Modern American Fiction*. Edinburgh. Edinburgh University Press.

Sappho (1992). *Poems and Fragments*, trans. J. Balmer. Newcastle upon Tyne: Bloodaxe Books.

Schulte, R. & Biguenet, J. (eds.) (1992). *Theories of Translation: An Anthology of Essays from Dryden to Derrida*. Chicago, IL: University of Chicago Press.

Scott, C. (2010). Re-theorizing the Literary in Literary Translation. In A. Fawcett, K. L. Guadarrama Garcia, & R. Hyde Parker, eds., *Translation: Theory and Practice in Dialogue*. Continuum Studies in Translation. London: Bloomsbury Publishing, pp. 109–27.

Shay, J. (1994). *Achilles in Vietnam: Combat Trauma and the Undoing of Character*. New York: Simon & Schuster.

Shay, J. (2002). *Odysseus in America: Combat Trauma and the Trials of Homecoming*. New York: Scribner.

Shelley, P. (2013). Hymn to Mercury, from Homer. In *Prometheus Unbound: A Lyrical Drama in Four* Acts, *with Other Poems*. Cambridge Library Collection – Fiction and Poetry. Cambridge: Cambridge University Press, pp. 821–54.

Simon, S. (1996). *Gender in Translation: Cultural Identity and the Politics of Transmission*. London: Routledge.

Slavitt, D. R. (trans.) (1994). *The* Metamorphoses *of Ovid: Freely Translated into Verse*. Baltimore, MD: Johns Hopkins University Press.

Smith, A. (2007). *Girl Meets Boy*. Canongate Myths 8. Edinburgh: Canongate.

Stallings, A. (2021). Like Sheep: On Translating a Literary Plague in a Time of Pandemic. *The Hudson Review* 73(4), 541–6.

Steiner, G. (1986). *Antigones: The Antigone Myth in Western Literature, Art, and Thought*. Oxford: Oxford University Press.

Steiner, G. (1996). Homer in English. In *No Passion Spent: Essays 1978–1996*. London: Faber and Faber, pp. 88–107.

Steiner, G. (2004). Homer in English Translation. In R. Fowler, ed., *The Cambridge Companion to Homer*. Cambridge: Cambridge University Press, pp. 363–75.

Stoppard, T. (2022). Introduction. In *Penelope*. London: Faber and Faber, pp. v–viii.

Talbot, S. (2004). English Ghosts of Callimachus. *Arion: A Journal of Humanities and the Classics*. Third Series, 12(1), 139–69.

Taplin, O. (2007). Some Assimilations of the Homeric Simile in Later Twentieth-Century Poetry. In B. Graziosi & E. Greenwood, eds., *Homer in the Twentieth Century: Between World Literature and the Western Canon*. Classical Presences. Oxford: Oxford University Press, pp. 177–90.

Tate, A. (1977). *Collected Poems 1919–1976*. New York: Farrar, Straus and Giroux.

Thomas, R. F. (2012). The Streets of Rome: The Classical Dylan. In W. Brockliss, P, Chaudhuri, A. Haimson Lushkov, & K. Wasdin, eds., *Reception and the Classics: An Interdisciplinary Approach to the Classical Tradition*. Cambridge: Cambridge University Press, pp. 134–59.

Trachsler, V. (2021). 'The Need for Translation': The Role of Translation in Eavan Boland's Work. *Translation and Literature* 30(1), 30–51.

Trinacty, C. (2016). Intertextual translation in Ovid, Seneca, and Ted Hughes. *Classical Receptions Journal* 8(4), 479–505.

Underwood. S. (1998). *English Translators of Homer: From George Chapman to Christopher Logue*. Plymouth: Northcote House and British Council.

Underwood, S. (2014). *Cold Calls*: The Penultimate Instalment of Logue's Homer. *New Voices in Classical Reception Studies* 9, 85–95. https://fass .open.ac.uk/sites/fass.open.ac.uk/files/files/new-voices-journal/issue9/under wood.pdf.

Vandiver, E. (2010). *Stand in the Trench, Achilles: Classical Receptions in British Poetry of the Great War*. Classical Presences. Oxford: Oxford University Press.

Venuti, L. (2004). *The Translation Studies Reader*, 2nd ed. London: Routledge.

Vergil (2008). *The Aeneid*, trans. S. Ruden. New Haven, CT: Yale University Press.

Vergil (2020). *The Aeneid*, trans. S. Bartsch. London: Profile Books.

Virgil (1971). *The Aeneid of Virgil*, trans. A. Mandelbaum. Berkeley: University of California Press.

Virgil (1981). *The Aeneid*, trans. R. Fitzgerald. New York: Random House.

Virgil ([1697] 1997). *Virgil's Aeneid*, trans. J. Dryden. Penguin Classics. Harmondsworth: Penguin Books.

Virgil (2005). *The Aeneid*, trans. S. Lombardo, ed. W. R. Johnson. Indianapolis, IN: Hackett Publishing.

Virgil (2006). *The Aeneid*, trans. R. Fagles. New York: Viking Penguin.

von Flotow, L. (1997). *Translation and Gender: Translating in the 'Era of Feminism'*. Perspectives on Translation Theories Explained. London: Routledge.

Walcott, D. (1990). *Omeros*. New York: Farrar, Straus and Giroux.

Warner, M. (2004). *Fantastic Metamorphoses, Other Worlds: Ways of Telling the Self*. Clarendon Lectures in English. Oxford: Oxford University Press.

Webb, T. (2004). Homer and the Romantics. In R. Fowler, ed., *The Cambridge Companion to Homer*. Cambridge: Cambridge University Press, pp. 287–310.

West, D. L. (2011). *The Making of the* Iliad: *Disquisition and Analytical Commentary*. Oxford: Oxford University Press.

Wilmer, S. E. (2007). Finding a Post-Colonial Voice for Antigone: Seamus Heaney's *Burial at Thebes*. In L. Hardwick & C. Gillespie, eds., *Classics in Post-Colonial Worlds*. Classical Presences. Oxford: Oxford University Press, pp. 228–44.

Wilson, E. (2009). Violent Grace: Anne Carson's *An Oresteia*. *The Nation*, 8 April. www.thenation.com/article/archive/violent-grace-anne-carsons-ores teia/.

Wilson, E. (2018). Translator's Note. In Homer, *The Odyssey*. New York: W. W. Norton, pp. 83–91.

Wilson, E. (2019). Epilogue: Translating Homer As a Woman. In F. Cox & E. Theodorakopoulos, eds., *Homer's Daughters: Women's Responses to Homer in the Twentieth Century and Beyond*. Classical Presences. Oxford: Oxford University Press, pp. 279–98.

Wilson, P. (2004). Homer and the English Epic. In R. Fowler, ed., *The Cambridge Companion to Homer*. Cambridge: Cambridge University Press, pp. 272–86.

Ziolkowski, T. (1993). *Virgil and the Moderns*. Princeton, NJ: Princeton University Press.

Žižek, S. (2016). *Antigone*. London: Bloomsbury Academic.

Zukofsky, C. & Zukofsky, L. (eds. & trans.) (1969). *Catullus (Gai Valeri Catulli Veronensis liber)*. London: Cape Golliard Press and Grossman Publishers.

Acknowledgements

Thanks are due to Kirsten Malmkjær, the series editor of Elements in Translation and Interpreting, for her encouragement and diligent counsel along the way. This Element greatly progressed while I was Fulbright Foundation fellow at the Department of Classics of The Ohio State University in the winter/spring of 2021 and from discussions with my academic hosts – Professor Gregory Jusdanis, in particular – during my stay at Columbus. *Creative Classical Translation* was developed further in late summer of 2021, while I was a visiting scholar at Downing College, Cambridge. I am grateful to Stanley Lombardo and Rachel Hadas for taking the time to be interviewed on aspects of their work (in the case of the latter, a published version of our conversation also appeared in the winter 2022 issue of *Literary Matters*). Further appreciation is owed to Lombardo and his co-editor, William Levitan, for granting me an early look at *Tales of Dionysus: The* Dionysiaca *of Nonnus of Panopolis* as this volume was being edited for publication in 2022; thanks also to Teresa Cotroneo for her assistance with proofreading; Maria-Venetia Kyritsi for help with sourcing some texts; and to the poet Richard Berengarten for our conversations near the River Cam.

About the Author

Paschalis Nikolaou is Associate Professor in Literary Translation at the Ionian University, Greece. His essays have appeared in several edited volumes, including most recently a co-written chapter on 'Translating Poetry' for *The Cambridge Handbook of Translation* (2022). His study *The Return of Pytheas: Scenes from British and Greek Poetry in Dialogue* was published in 2017.

Cambridge Elements ≡

Translation and Interpreting

Cambridge Elements $\equiv$

Translation and Interpreting

Printed in the United States
by Baker & Taylor Publisher Services